still alive!

still alive!

a temporary condition

a memoir

herbert gold

arcade publishing • new york

FIRST EDITION

Chapters of this book appeared, in different versions, in *Commentary, Hudson Review, Michigan Quarterly Review, Midstream,* and *Republic of Letters.*

Library of Congress Cataloging-in-Publication Data
Gold, Herbert, 1924–
   Still alive! : a temporary condition / Herbert Gold. —1st ed.
     p. cm.
  ISBN 978-1-55970-870-8 (alk. paper)
  1. Gold, Herbert, 1924– 2. Authors, American—20th century—
Biography. 3. Bohemianism. I. Title.
  PS3557.O34Z46 2008
  813'.54—dc22
  [B]   2007040636

Published in the United States by Arcade Publishing, Inc., New York
Distributed by Hachette Book Group USA

Visit our Web site at www.arcadepub.com

10 9 8 7 6 5 4 3 2 1

Designed by API

EB

PRINTED IN THE UNITED STATES OF AMERICA

For Sid
In memory

The ancient domino player in the only café in town appeared for his game every day. He was said to be over a hundred years old. Asked if he was the oldest person in Jacmel, he answered, "Oh no, Monsieur. There are many who are older than I am, but they are all dead."

—Hans Christoph Buch,
Ombres dansantes, ou Le Zombie c'est moi

Approaching the conclusion of our span, matters are dire. We can't take it personally. Though matters are dire, memory and comedy continue. The Intelligent Designer, if there is one, must be a malicious joker.

Who are we to pretend to better character?

—Rev. Reuben Gracchus, *Guide to the Perplexed 2*

contents

This is a book about aging—how time overtakes us, how memory, loss, hope, joy, pain, success, failure, the lifelong accumulation of events and dreams crowd about us with every new day. How we change what we once were into what we are now. How the years pass, and we get to where we're going. How recognition of the comic and tragic miracle of this temporary condition, our lives, helps us get through.

I've looked at my own address for an accounting. Out of courtesy, some names and circumstances have been altered.

still alive!

1

Remembrance of Cultural Revolutions Past

Direct from the People's Republic of China she came with the glad tidings!

We were invited to gather at the apartment of our friends the Natters to hear Myrtle Ferguson describe her experience at the center of the Cultural Revolution about which so many lies were being told in the imperialist bourgeois media. Myrtle taught English in a Beijing school; she wore a monochrome uniform like millions of her fellow strugglers; her hair, brutally cropped, fell over her forehead in a slab no one would dare call bangs. She was traveling in Amerika on a tour of enlightenment, sent with the full authority of the Authorities. Zucchini and Monterey Jack cheese would be served, along with wine. At my request, beer for me.

Piled democratically together on the floor, leaning on giant Esalen pillows, clutching our wine and cheese and sliced zucchini (beer, me), we turned our yearning faces toward oblong Myrtle, standing in her high-collared suit in front of the fireplace. Flirtation and gossip were shushed by our host. We were ready to be instructed.

"My former parents in Swarthmore, that's Pennsylvania, tried to mold me into someone like them, an Amerikan female," Myrtle bitterly confessed. We all knew, thanks to her clipped and crunched pronunciation of the word "Amerikan," that there was a *k* in there, counteracting our indoctrination by misogynist, patriarchal schooling. "I came to understand my destiny lay in the People's Republic, home to the Chinese people. In the East, land of the mighty Red River. . . ." After the groundwork, she got into the more advanced stuff: ". . . so I took a job teaching English in . . ." Articulated by Myrtle in a doubtlessly authentic People's Republic accent, the word "Beijing" sounded to my ears like amplified granola.

Wind chimes rang out in the evening fog on Russian Hill in San Francisco. Myrtle had brought the chimes as a house present for her hosts, Marjie and Ted Natter. The bringing of house presents was another gracious custom she had learned in the People's Republic.

These were days that tried persons' souls. Cadre Myrtle was resolute, stern of demeanor. Once upon a time, far away, in a place dominated by brutal patriarchal Quakers, they had taught her to be meek and mild, but she managed to escape their cruel manipulations. It was a clean getaway. Unlike erroneous seekers, she had found the truth and intended to share it. The room was crowded. I leaned with my wife against the legs of a couple who had taken the couch. Our friend, Ted Natter, borrowed the neck of my beer bottle for tapping purposes and asked that we discontinue all private whisperings. There was an endless war in Viet Nam, Amerikans were out of step with history, and discussions of chardonnay versus pinot noir should stop immediately.

My teeth bit down hard and satisfyingly on a crisp vertical slice of zucchini. I licked a slippery cube of Monterey Jack. I offered my wife the first chance at my second beer, and she delicately swallowed from the long neck. I loved her every gesture.

Stalwart, serene, and committed to her mission, Myrtle was describing how the People settled a troubling question about the principal of the school where she taught. "The masses entered his office and we determined that he had a landlord mentality which he had craftily hidden from everyone."

Although uncertain if this conformed to the rules, I raised my hand.

"Crafty and deceitful," she was saying, "like all those with landlord mentalities —"

I waved my arm. She ignored the disturbance. Unfortunately, in my eagerness to speak, I spread a mist of beer over our dear neighbors on the floor. Melissa, my well-mannered wife, prudently removed the bottle from my foam-covered hand. "How?" I asked Myrtle. "How did you find out about his landlord mentality?"

"The masses looked into his desk. We opened a drawer."

But they didn't harm him, she explained, because the masses understood that this was not the way of the Great Leader. I murmured, not even certain what I was saying. The masses, in their just desire for reeducation of cadre gone astray, asked the landlord-mentality school principal to sit in the courtyard with a dunce cap on his head; then the masses urinated on him. The masses lined up in orderly fashion to express their sincere outrage and urge him to reform his thought. I believe what I was murmuring was a question about whether the bladder-voiding method of reeducation enlisted both students and teachers, or perhaps it was merely to clear up a technical detail about how the female masses positioned themselves if they remained standing. Revolutionaries, of course, can find a way, even as the turbulent waters of People's Republic springtime rains rush down the slopes of the mountains, finding the correct channels.

Having murmured, I spoke aloud. "Did he reform?"

Myrtle Ferguson, the repentant Quaker from Swarthmore, regretted that the answer remained uncertain. Having taken the capitalist road, the principal chose to commit suicide. He made this decision without consulting his colleagues, typical behavior of capitalist roaders. It was a landlord mentality characteristic to deprive the people of their labor.

Our guest of honor was a seeker of the righteous path, as were most of us. In the future, she might be kind, and so might the masses, but today, this year, this century, there was no time for weakness.

I could have used another long-necked bottle to share with my wife. Ted Natter sought me out during the post-lesson group discussion; socializing was not on the program tonight. He suspected that I was the victim of my own landlord mentality, a recent perpetrator of murmurings. He sought to rescue me by Socratic, or perhaps Hegelian, interrogation. He asked: Was I opposed to culture?

No.

Was I opposed to revolution?

Uh . . . depends.

He ignored this. So Cultural and Revolution, you put them together, and you get Synergy, two conjoined, unbeatable mighty goods. "Look at yourself, Herb. Look at history."

I looked at myself and history, now located in an apartment in San Francisco. Peace picketers (I too was one), red Mao buttons (well, Melissa had sewn rainbow ribbons on my shirts), and Earth shoes were on the march. I noticed cartridge belts with bullets on some of the more stylish women and asked one, whom I'll call Trenda (not her real name), why. "It's a neat look," she said. Later she would explain in detail: "Edgy. Pushes the envelope."

No bourgeois exploiters with landlord mentalities were being shipped from post–Summer of Love San Francisco to work on pig farms in, say, New Jersey or Tennessee. Along with Maui Wowie, Little Red Books were being imported to expand the consciousness of sliced-zucchini-nibbling, wine-sipping exploiters (me, beer) on Russian, Nob, and Telegraph hills, and also in Pacific Heights.

Ted Natter had recently taken to reminding Melissa: "Why don't you tell Herb to stay home and look after the children so you can go out and write books?" She gazed at him and explained, with that generous smile, which usually removed the sting from her messages: "He does what he does and I do what I do. And we have nice babysitters, this Filipino and tonight this girl from the Art Institute —"

"*Woman*, not girl. Filipina, not with an *o*. But hiring *slaves* doesn't —"

We'd had our beverages, our cheese and zucchini, and our lecture, and it was time to walk back home, saving an hour off the cost of our slave. Often the best part of an evening out was the stroll home in the San Francisco damp, Melissa's hand on my arm, letting the evening settle silent around us.

Love Thy Sisters

Like so many of my age in San Francisco during that space of glorious Unreality Check, I had been reinfected with adolescence, but doing it better this time, giddy with the music (the "San Francisco Sound!"), the dancing, the avid gaze of the young as they (we!) danced, grokked (?), & grooved, and read Hermann Hesse for life guidance. Well, burdened with judgments I couldn't quite overcome, I made an exception for Hesse on the grounds of excess mysticism, for Chairman Mao on other grounds, but not for the Jefferson Airplane, the Grateful Dead, the Beatles, and even Country Joe with his "gimme an *F*" antiphonal chant against the Viet Nam war. Goddamn, but it was fun. Blessed indeed was it to be alive in Golden Gate Park, including the Panhandle. Was that eucalyptus I smelled, or was it smokable banana peels? Space travelers who had no need of NASA equipment launched themselves from Hippie Hill day and night, bongos and guitars providing gentle and soothing jet propulsion.

During a season or two, the new world began promptly on Monday or any other day when the troops of the children's crusade climbed off the Greyhound from Galveston, Ithaca, or Cleveland. I was already here, smelling the flowers, the patchouli, the eucalyptus, and my wife's hair. We consented to be very young, very happy. Although "digging ze scene," as a hitchhiking French hippie said, practicing her San Francisco–speak, I also — not *really* an adolescent — dug narrowing my eyes and inscribing judgments.

The lament that youth is wasted on the young was newly scored for electric guitars. Now youth could be wasted on everyone; love oh love oh careless love. We looked deeply into each other, often seeing only ourselves, but sometimes, yes sometimes, seeing the other. Nearly twenty years earlier, sprung into civilian life after three years in the U.S. Army, I had stumbled into a marriage that began with low-level guerilla warfare and ended in an all-out scorched-earth campaign. But as sometimes happens, suffering was not absolute. There was survival; there were two daughters after the term of warfare. And now here was Melissa, loving to my daughters, who returned her care with adoration. I was young again; Melissa was still young. We brought into this new world the three children we wanted, all in a row.

The ecology of Eden would not be complete without apples and snakes. The democracy of flowerdom contained elements of an unfree command economy. Timothy Leary preached both freedom and psychedelic prescriptions, and covertly dosed his visitors' drinks. Our friends the Natters intended to change the nature of marriage in general and our own in particular. Truth trumpeters, truth activists, Marjie and Ted believed that the marriage of Melissa and me required drastic reform. Unmet requirements were a challenge to them, especially in a time that demanded change "by any means necessary," as a pithy Black Panther put it.

They launched a lightning campaign to save our souls. Foremost on the program was that child and household duties must be moved from the wife to the spouse. The writing trade needed to be transferred to the wife. Once these matters were settled, more would come up.

Unfortunately, we balked at reform. I continued practicing prose; Melissa believed it was her own choice to spend much of the day with our children, who wore gender-specific clothing except for diapers. Marjie and Ted had their work cut out for them.

"Companionship" is a word derived from an idea meaning "the sharing of bread." Our friendship with the Natters might have become monotonous except that monotony was not allowed in this time of the Summer of Love hangover. Although Ted was pinched in judgment and vindictive when disagreed with, and Marjie was virulent in her anger at what violated each turn in her evolving code, they both had wide, generous, bright, and happy smiles. That's almost the same as having large, generous, accepting hearts.

Melissa and I thought to rescue a friendship "by any means necessary," even a bourgeois dinner involving candles, wine, and normal conversation about children, psychedelics, and the War in Viet Nam.

Ted and Marjie were happy to join us, making a seminar of four, not even asking first who did the cooking. Our own last-ditch campaign, envisioning light at the end of a tunnel of dissonance, included rack of lamb, brown rice, and a salad that included baby shrimp and a delicate vinaigrette dressing, which Melissa included partly so she could pronounce it like the waiter at our favorite North Beach restaurant: "vinegaret." Sometimes her jokes were tainted by elitism.

The feeding neared its mellow yet fraught conclusion with crème brûlée prepared from a secret recipe Melissa had inherited from her mother and promised to give to nobody except her own daughter. We bit the crisp caramel, we licked the high-cholesterol spoons. Marjie put her hand on my wife's hipbone and announced: "We can only destroy patriarchal control of Amerika if we learn to love our sisters."

This was not a stab at learning the secret recipe for crème brûlée. This was a Pass.

Melissa's delicate Celtic skin turned purple with embarrassment, both because of the theoretical and argumentative nature of the pass and also because of the respective husbands witnessing the event. The passee moved away. The hand was detached, it slipped off. There was a difficult moment of silence.

As a typical misogynist sexist host, it was my duty to say or do something. "Uh," I said. And then: "So, Ted, what do you think about this?"

His voice, normally high, rose almost to a treble clef, as if his chest had tightened. "I totally respect it," he said.

"Do you want to love your brothers, too, uh, that way?"

"I do, I do! Problem is . . . you wouldn't be up for sharing the experience with me? Most of my friends have bought into the straight thing. And the kind of man I could pick up —"

He read my mind. I was thinking of the cluster of Polk Street hustlers near Hard On Leathers, Gray Wolf Clothing, and a bar, The White Swallow. The Castro was just being colonized.

"— that kind, it would be, I don't know, sort of like uncomfortable?"

Right. It took two to tango, even this theoretical tango, this tango in the portion of the cortex that measures moral imperatives. "Someday," I said, and he gazed expectantly into my eyes, "someday we'll have to not talk about this."

The evening ended with insincere vows all around to meet again soon. I told Melissa that I loved the way she blushed a deep purple, because I could never provide such a dramatic portrayal of embarrassment, due to my darker skin. "We Scottish-Irish-English have all the luck, don't we?" she said. She sighed. Our friendship with the Natters seemed to be suspended.

Nevertheless, in the metropolitan village of San Francisco, we met and remet. That's the deal, one of the peculiar advantages of living in a metropolis with all its eccentricities and dangers, like a space station on earth, and also in a village with its proximities and interconnections. During an afternoon espresso run at Caffe Trieste, flagship of the Beat flotilla, now beached among tourists, memories, and a few stray boheems, I found Ted also taking an afternoon espresso. Great minds do not always think alike; not all minds are great; but espresso is a valuable common lubricator. We moved our chairs to sit together. Instead of commenting on the niceness of the weather and the steamy warmth of the Trieste, I asked Ted if he thought Marjie had developed in recent years some kind of suspicion of men. "Oh, no," he declared, defending her consistency. "It's long-standing. Not me, of course, we're super-close."

"I know you're an exception. But why the hatred of other men?"

He struggled for a succinct explanation that would not delay our return to spouses and children. "Well, she's studied history. Hitler was a man."

Aristotle was a friend of mine (not him personally, but his writings); the syllogism implied here lay beyond my grasp. I tried to think, *Q.E.D.* It didn't work. I tried to think, *Therefore* . . . Still no luck.

Ted hastened to assure me that it was nothing personal

and remedy was available. Ever since they decided not to be husband and wife but spouse and spouse, equal, level, parallel, and sharing, all discord had evaporated from their partnership. He agreed to clothe their two sons in dresses so that they would appreciate what women face in the patriarchal world. She compromised on one matter. They were allowed to urinate standing up if they insisted.

"Copacetic with you, Spouse?" she had asked.

"Cool, Spouse," he answered.

They didn't eat grapes (César Chávez). They sewed their own rainbow flag to hang at the door (gay rights). They chose Halloween as their major holiday because witches can be of any gender, no matter what prejudiced people think.

Later, Spouse and Spouse got divorced anyway.

The family therapist whom Marjie, now mostly Marjoe, consulted asked her, "Do you want to split?" and Marjoe said yes, so the family therapist said, "Well, that means you're fine, so off you go, sister." It was a divorce of the new No Fault variety and of the even newer Everybody Wins persuasion. They still shared picketings, marches, and custody of the sons, who objected to their dresses, although their father referred to them as caftans. On the playground during soccer practice, fellow students sneered at linguistic distinctions.

My wife with her well-exercised love of comedy proposed to me that she invite Marjie's ex-husband on a date. This was an idea in accord with the times; it also commented on the Natters' particular abstract theories. Melissa telephoned Ted and he was thrilled. "Lunch?" she asked.

He started to name a time when he would drive over for her. She interrupted. "I'll pick *you* up," she said.

That was the drill. It was 1972, after all. Only sexists of

the fifties and earlier would expect the XY chromosome zygotes to come for the XX chromosome zygotes. In the terrible history of oppressive social conditioning, men had usurped sexual vehicle transport privileges.

Melissa giggled; I chortled, being an XY chromosome zygote non-giggler.

On the appointed day she arrived at Ted's door with a corsage to pin on his Mao jacket, which was worn over a Mexican shirt, green illicit herb embroidery sprouting behind the live legal gardenias she pinned to him. He stood stiffly at attention. She didn't stab his chest.

"Relax," she commanded nervous Ted. Later, at the Good Karma Café, she whispered loudly to the waiter to be sure to give her the check. Ted had trouble relaxing. Sometimes grooviness was asking a lot, even of a cutting-edge thinker. She did not make advances to him because he had difficulty adjusting to Marjie's multicultural, polyamorous principles. He may also have been suspicious of Melissa's sudden embrace of them.

No damage to our household except for the price of lunch. American civilization did not take an immediate correct turn, the Viet Nam war did not end at once, the borders of expectation between the sexes, now called genders, did not dissolve over the arugula salads. But every little bit counted.

Melissa came home, still giggling, me chortling, our children that evening reflecting our good humor for the normal mysterious reasons of children.

Nevertheless, family stress occurs in general, and in the early seventies, with three babies in diapers, a fifteen-month space between our daughter and our twin sons, stress occurred in particular in our family. The times were ones of marital breakdowns between the XX chromosome folks and the XY chromosome people. This was not new, but the intensity of it was special. My wife's history was that of a well-brought-up Ivy League young woman; most of her friends came from similar backgrounds, academically replete, trained winners. Their husbands were the same. But one by one, the marriages were cracking. I would appear at the end of the afternoon, and she would say, "Muffie has left Glenn." A month or two later, Polly departed her marriage with Devon.

It felt ominous. When the fourth pal danced off in her Capezios, I was relieved, cosmically, superstitiously, and referred to the group as the Four Horsewomen of the Apocalypse. Then there was a fifth. There was a sixth, a seventh. In each case, the bereft husband seemed not to be a brute, conspicuously unfaithful, an alcoholic, or a negligent provider. He was a husband; that was the problem.

The eighth horsewoman of the Apocalypse was Melissa.

Being a reasonable person, generous and fair-minded, she agreed to see a therapist. She was sad about my sadness. She was considering our children, too. The therapist recommended by one of her friends lived in outer Marin, but she made the drive anyway. One session was all the treatment necessary, since she entered the office and the psychologist asked what was the problem, and she said, "I want to leave my husband." The therapist looked warmly into her eyes. "Well, then you're okay," she said.

My wife returned grinning with the information. We adjourned to the bedroom. She noted that this therapist had been divorced three times and confided that she thought she might be more fond of women than of men. She shrugged. "Those are the breaks, Herb."

For a while, Former Spouse Marjoe tried to promote an educational program in "teledildonics." This was a way to use mind control to move imaginary dildos in desired rhythms from a distance. Marshall McLuhan advocated "probes," and after all, a probe that didn't work out was just as good as one that did. It was still a probe. But when the course failed to draw paying registrants, she moved on to tending bar in the Diana the Huntress Café on Valencia Street.

I have changed some details in this history to protect the unisex identities of everyone but my former wife and me. No actual derogation of telekinesis, the science of moving things around by mental power, is intended. In any case, Spouse and Spouse Natter are not into the linear activity of reading words ordered by patriarchal grammar. That was so last century. "Whatever," as their sons, now adults, like to say. But all who are offended, wherever you are, can lift my fingers from the typewriter keys and slap my hands.

This was a time, the seventies, of bad sideburns, bad fabrics, bad disco revolving balls, and also bad politics. Most times seem to be times of bad politics; lava lamps were unique. The sixties flower world of love, psychedelics, Viet Nam protest, self-discovery, and "I hear you" as the proper response to disagreement had devolved into the irritable hangover of the seventies.

After friendship with the Natters and also my marriage ended, I happened to enter a Just Desserts café in San Francisco where a group of women sat near the door. One of them had seen me coming and covered her face with her hands, even spreading her fingers to hide her hairline. As I passed, she removed her hands from her face and announced accusingly, startling everyone in the vicinity: "You don't even recognize women, do you, Herb?"

"I didn't see you, Marjie."

Triumphantly she said: "No, of course you wouldn't."

Valiant Marjie-Marjoe was like the only woman admitted to the French Foreign Legion, fighting for distant causes, attaining glory and obscure results "by any means necessary," including hiding her face in Just Desserts. Probably that's not how she saw herself. At times she even ventured to compromise her principles, as when she kept the mole on her nose, only plucking the single dark hair that grew from it.

I recognize anger, emotion recollected in non-Wordsworthian tranquility, during an effort to recapture a history which seemed to pass under the gypsy's curse: "May you live in interesting times." I recall both my mother's stern stare at the thought of those who disappointed her and my father's stubborn calm because he knew how to survive and so many others didn't. My adolescent rage against my parents, fleeing as a seventeen-year-old toward wherever my hitchhiking thumb would take me — freedom, someplace else, even if I needed to steal milk and bread from doorsteps — now is transformed into gratitude. I remember my mother and father with love. I learned strictness and stubbornness from them. I also learned anger, malice, and vindictiveness, now freely manifested.

Someday, probably in fifty or sixty years, I won't nurse my resentments. We must mature, forgive, achieve serenity and true peace.

Have fifty or sixty years passed yet?

My sons and daughters will pass on to their children the soul melodies and dissonances of their own mother and father; and their children in turn will continue the enterprise forever. Like all of us, I think of myself as an individual, navigating alone in the universe, but I'm also a moment in history, a point of transmission.

Now and then, there's a brusque interruption of the gradual slide into the fate of all living creatures. A tooth needs to be pulled as soon as possible. A cataract needs to be peeled off. During these times, the slide seems precipitous. But hey, the tooth is out and the fresh plastic implanted in healthy bone ("Very fortunate at your age," says the oral surgeon). The cloudy lens in the eye is replaced by the latest advance in ophthalmology ("Good as new, maybe better," says the expert, "and Medicare covers most of it"). Good again, good as new! Until, maybe, tomorrow.

The leaves of the calendar drop, the snows melt, the potholes grow deeper. (No snow in San Francisco, however.) I decided to invite Ted for lunch to revisit our shared past. No longer married to Marjie, he is also no longer married to his next wife. His grown sons no longer wear dresses, unless during secret fashion shows before bedroom mirrors in their suburban tract houses. Ted's hair is still ample, but fluffy and white. He has passed through his spasm of Maoism and his longing to share polyamorous sex with the proper same-gender partner.

I buy the lunch; no corsage. With my purchase, I assume the right to ask questions. Beginning abstractly in order to ease gracefully into my personal concerns, I bring up the People's Republic of China. "Well, it didn't work out," he says. He shrugs. The broken eggs didn't make a viable omelet or even a tasty egg foo yung. "Also, now they've got a lot of . . ." He considered how much to grant me. "Pollution?"

He still ends sentences with an upward-swinging question, in the California manner.

So then, cautiously, I bring up my marriage, declaring that of course I don't exactly blame him for causing trouble — the trouble went deeper into both character and the times than anything the Natters were responsible for — but I suggest that *bad will* hurts friendship.

Distressed, concerned, very much like a person who regretted accepting a free lunch, he said, "Well, Herb, you were a sexist, you know." He gathered defensive momentum: "You wrote all those books, but Melissa didn't get to write any. Who knows if, instead, you . . ."

What?

". . . if the world had been different?"

He too had regrets. He too had lost a few things. He picked at his non-farmgrown salmon. Writing books is a dream for many; even Ted has written a couple of prescriptive manuals; and Marjie had formed a publishing house with her "womyn" partner to issue their works of feminist antirevisionism.

"So how are the kids?" he asked.

He took the words right out of my mouth. "Fine, how are yours?" And once more we vowed to meet again before too long because time passes so quickly and a shared history must be respected and, after all, we used to be friends. No one pronounced the word "misogynist," and only I pronounced the phrase "Cultural Revolution."

Not Letting Go

And so, although we had insincerely promised that we would meet again, we actually did.

Nostalgia may, like jealousy, do no good work, but remembrance provides the necessary fuel for taking stock. Once more I invited Ted Natter for coffee, lunch, or dinner, his choice. My telephoned heartiness seemed to make him cautious. "Coffee," he said.

As we settled in at the café, I reminded him that the price of coffee had gone up. That's what I remembered; he remembered that they didn't have fair-trade coffee in those days. We fell into a moment of silent communion over dissonant memories, but we both recalled the pretty German hippie who used to serve the coffee and her proud display of American idiom skills —"gut vibez," "hup tight," "Miles Davidtz."

We were two old friends whose friendship had been a casualty of the times. The bond of dead friendship is still a bond — shared memories and mis-memories. I told him about the Weatherperson who visited me to ask for money, seeming to offer her comely person as a door prize. Also, the Maoist of the Revolutionary Communist Party, Splinter Faction Direct Action Committee — not precisely its real name — a City and County of San Francisco social worker, who came to ask for a contribution for Bob Avakian, Chairman-in-Exile. Subcommander Helen did not offer sex or even hint at it. Perhaps I wasn't her type, or perhaps all her erotic needs were satisfied by the Maximum Leader and Designated Guide-in-Exile, now carrying on from the 13th Arrondissement in Paris. "Bob has read your works," she had said. "He thinks you're salvageable."

I made herbal tea for the visitor. She examined the tag at the end of the teabag string to make certain it didn't come from imperialist highlands. I didn't offer my visitor a joint, because I couldn't guarantee that the marijuana wasn't grown by reactionary forces. Unlike the comely Weatherperson who had made her approach with flirtatious charm, a hint of quid pro quo, this young social worker cleaved doggedly to her teacup and her Bob Avakian mission.

"When the kulaks and the counterrevolutionaries are crushed like cucarachas under the feet of the working people, you will have a chance to appeal." Her promise called to mind the Chinese school principal with the landlord mentality. In the future, her offer of an appeal might not be repeated.

Oh, where are you now, young civil service employee and destroyer of the oligarchy? The workers and peasants of the San Francisco Bay Area cry out for you.

Subcommander Helen may have a civil service pension and grandchildren by this time. Ted listened attentively to my account, letting me ramble. We had lived a history together.

"Yeah, that Avakian faction," he said. "I think I knew that activist. She have a Frida Kahlo decal on her Corvair?"

"She came by bike."

"Was it a ten-speed?"

Details, details. I didn't remember everything.

19

After his stint as a Russian Hill Maoist, Ted had settled into the job of ameliorating the world's ills on a freelance basis. Frontal opposition seemed counterproductive; it was better to save the whales incrementally, one by one, and then move on to the dolphins, the prairie dogs, the chickens in pens. His metaphor about needing to break eggs in order to make omelets was no longer at the top of the agenda for either Ted or Lenin. In these times, inoperative, like Stalin and Mao. But unlike them, Ted still wanted to help. He wrote mailings for a foundation opposed to child labor and shark fishing, the whales being saved by others. It wasn't a change of direction; it was an evolution. "I'm doing a job," he said, "and I'm doing it good."

This sounded like a slogan he had developed in order to get the attention of honest folks confused by the uses of "well" and "good." He was still getting down with the masses.

Now that he was no longer married —"between marriages," as he said — and his child support days were over, the living was pretty easy. (The sons, now in trousers, were doing okay for themselves: one a chef, the other a middle school teacher.) He rented a bachelor apartment with cotton balls in a glass jar, a stack of *The Nation* on an end table (no copies of *Gourmet*), shampoo and conditioner from a worker-owned store on a convenient shelf in the shower. He has earned his comfort. No more cockroaches. A cat. A Spanish-speaking cleaning woman comes every two weeks, checks the cat box, changes the sheets, dusts and vacuums, and what he doesn't know about her legal status hurts neither of them.

He remembered my advising him that boric acid in kitchen cracks seemed to take care of East Coast cockroaches; it stuck to their legs, they carried it into their nests, it ate away at their siblings. "That was repulsive, Herb," he said, "so New York. Now we chase them out with ultrasound."

No longer a revolutionary, Ted was an evolutionary. The suffering urge for female companionship had also faded, calmed by regular coin insertion into the jukebox at the Puccini Café, which stocks music from *Turandot* and *La Bohème* and gives a fellow between marriages his space for sentimental meditation.

And that stuff about wanting, if he could, to be bisexual?

"You remember that, Herb?"

"I do."

"That was just, I don't know, Marjie thought it was part of the program. Like McLuhan said, it was a probe."

Midlife tristesse has replaced indignation as his driving force. He wears a fine halo of white hair, and without actually losing weight, his cheekbones are more visible. There is a touch of haggardness. He apologized for the hoarseness of his voice. "I get acid reflux, you know, fried food," he explained, "and I ran out of Tums last night." He has found something else to believe in — calcium carbonate in an over-the-counter formulation.

Consistent with my normal kindliness, I asked if his activities on behalf of the Cultural Revolution had been funded by . . . "Are you a man of dependent means?"

"Pardon?"

"I mean, do you have . . . your parents left you a little something?"

"Herb, that's a low blow. Nothing major at all. A little house in, what difference does it make? But some, yes, so I did feel I needed to pay back."

After a proper silence in his view apartment above

North Beach, during mutual staring into the middle distance, we were recalling that last family dinner together. We were both embarrassed for me that I dwelled on the subject. I consoled him by saying that now Marjie's public pass at my wife, in the presence of husbands, seemed to have the purity of heroic theory. Although it was doomed to rebuff and purple blushing, it achieved its real goal as demonstration. And when Ted had said, "I'd like to, but I just can't . . . can't find the right man," he had proven he was not yet pure enough. There were still obstacles in the way of sex employed as a political statement. It came down to a traditional problem — Ted just didn't want sex with a man. He was still the selfish victim of personal desires. For Marjie, whether she desired or not, whether she had an appetite or not, was irrelevant. She was proving a point. She was making a revolutionary gesture. If necessary, mucous membranes could be lubricated by handy household products.

Like many fanatics, Marjie was consistent. When she hid her face and accused me of sexism for not recognizing her, she had won another victory over reality. She burned with the heat that enabled her to put dresses on her sons, who had been boisterous and charming kids, kicking a soccer ball in their encumbering skirts. What other people called "love" was, for Marjie, a continuation of the war, and not merely the war between the sexes. It was a war against imperfection in the world, a struggle to the death, which of course is the final perfection where all are equal.

The More Things Change . . . The More They Change

Peggy, a freelance seeker who left part of her cerebral cortex on pawn with the LSD dealer, had a revelation, had quite a few of them, and took up a new profession as seer of all things, past and future. She brought her tarot cards to the apartment where I was living with Melissa, then my wife-to-be, and offered her a reading, free of any charge. She shuffled the cards, turned one over, perhaps another, mumbled, and pronounced: "A tall red-headed man will be most important in your life."

"But," Melissa said, "I'm going to marry Herb and he isn't so tall or red haired."

"Those are mere details," said Peggy. "But hey, congratulations."

Of course the cards must have meant me. I was of upper medium height, and black is just a short jump from red on the color spectrum.

Despite their historical grooviness, the gone days of go-with-the-flow, the dancing in Golden Gate Park with the fragrance of fresh-smoked grass wafting above, the Natters' passion had not been to leap into the youth carnival as it then found us. Rather, they intended to control the world's unruliness with theory. For them, the necessary discipline could be achieved by surrendering control to a roster of distant perfect controllers, such as Chairman Mao or, in moments of hectic inspiration . . . Germaine Greer?

Melissa and I may have thought we were immune to nonsense because we were entertained by the fads, by what everyone now calls the herd of independent minds, but we too breathed that air. Restlessness was seductive, the sweet sounds of young voices raised to invoke Alice when she was ten feet tall; it was contagious. Add the scent of eucalyptus and patchouli; add eyeballs revolving with intimations of permanent youth and infinite pleasure; to experience the intoxication of the endless Summer of Love, you didn't even need the eucalyptus.

The shaven-headed militant who ran the Institute for the Study of Non-Violence for Joan Baez in the Carmel Valley argued with me on behalf of absolute and unconditional pacifism, which included not striking back in the case of assault on the street. Although impressed by his bravery, his venturing into the city on behalf of peace, I invoked the unreliable nature of mammals (he yawned) and asked if he would use force to stop a rape.

He gave this a long pretend-think. He had a sense of drama. Silent indignation bathed over us. He extended a finger and began to probe into the muscles of my shoulder while slowly, with stately emphasis, asking: "Why. Don't. You. Realize. Only. Pacifism. Can?" and so on.

His finger unerringly searched out nerves in my shoulder that were news to me. I squirmed away. "Hey! Ouch! Stop!"

It was another victory for the command center of nonviolence in the Carmel Valley. Joan Baez, that long-haired dark beauty, La Pasionaria of the Beat generation, is still singing, but the peace institute has finished its work and her hair is stylishly short and gray. She has dared to reveal previously concealed secrets about herself, including that she has a sense of humor and would really like a good record deal. Her staff pacifist has found other employment.

In the early seventies it seemed that every well-brought-up sensible woman was growing less sensible and less married. An entitled Old San Francisco hippie, with whom I sometimes carpooled to school functions and other childcare duties, reproached me for writing for *Playboy* magazine.

"Herb, that is a disgrace. You must stop. You owe it to yourself."

Her VW van was painted with flowers and mandalas. "Donna, I have five children to support. I can't do it writing for *The American Scholar*."

"You could try."

"You don't understand. You have a tax-free income of over a hundred thousand a year."

She was driving indignantly now, knuckles white on the steering wheel. "Herb, that is a dirty rotten lie. Ninety-seven thousand."

"Plus a house without a mortgage on Telegraph Hill."

She was driving indignantly and indignantly preparing her answer. She was used to being understood by men, or at least seeing men furrow their brows with the effort or the pretense of understanding, because she was not only rich and Old San Francisco, but also cute. Her dark glossy hair, sliced into bangs over her forehead, shortened her face, making the large round blue eyes appear even rounder, bluer, more mysteriously babylike in their rarely blinking gaze. Such eyes are an important ingredient in the will of many men, even liberated ones, to understand or pretend to understand.

"But I do all the cooking," she said.

Her parents had a resident cook; she did without. Her parents drove a white Cadillac. She drove a VW van with flower decals. Her husband was a lawyer, but on weekends he wore a buckskin jacket with Indian fringes. Eventually, of course, she too joined the horsewomen of the Apocalypse and lit out for the territory ahead, which in her case meant keeping the house and trust fund in the divorce settlement, but shaving her pubic hair in the shape of a heart. (How do I know this? *Everybody* knew this.)

The reason our world is filled with peace and love today is that Donna kept the faith.

After the unending Summer of Love ended, foreboding clouds gathered over the Autumn of Love, and folks were feeling angry in addition to groovy — irritated about parking meters, speed bumps, writers selling out to *Playboy*; mad about the justice system, not enough or too much affirmative action, abuse of food stamps; they were angry about not really ruling their own lives, as they had planned, after a season in which Free was the mantra. Sexual differences and gender confusions, pollutants in the tuna fish, tomatoes artificially ripened with blasts of chlorine gas — there was an all-ya-can buffet of life details to incite doubt about recently adopted truths. The Cultural Revolution turned out not to be so cultural, the revolution was a retrogression in both kindness and food supply. Directions for installing new electronic equipment were too confusing; hangovers lasted too long.

Were these concerns so unlike the griefs of their obsolete parents? The children of the Love generation, who had said, "No, no!" so sweetly during the Terrible Twos, were now heading toward the truly terrible sullenness of adolescence.

The final bell has not yet tolled for most of these friends of early middle age, when rock 'n' roll had not yet finished doing its damage to the ears of a generation. But if it hasn't tolled, it's tinkled a little in the wind. Groovy had its price. Men now wake at night to trudge toward the bathroom. New causes are no longer allowed to be called "crusades." Women have declared either victory over the patriarchy or that postmodern version of victory, defeat.

Where are the flower folks now? Some live in Bolinas. A few cashed out before the dot-com crash and are tending to gated estates in Silicon Valley. Some, alas, have moved off this earth without making clear where they were headed. The former Jesuit, former lawyer, formerly married man who now teaches English in China is not studying the teachings of Chairman Mao. He is in the People's Republic because he wants to study the teachings of dewy Chinese maidens who have left the farm and hope to meet American former lawyers, former Jesuits, former husbands in the big city. A shy swain, my friend blushes and timidly tries, with the correct tones, to pronounce the Chinese words for "You are the cutest little thing I ever did see." He's a Mandarin cowboy, grieving only because they don't serve brown rice in twenty-first-century China.

Donna is a doting grandmother with a succession of much younger lovers to dote with her when she takes the kids to Christmas productions of *The Nutcracker*. The hair is still glossy and black, the eyes very blue, the skin of her face unlined. She keeps the faith, lives the dream. Her well-managed trust has kept up with inflation. Untouched by gray, but glowing with a mysterious purple radiance, her hair needs no chemical assistance to shorten her forehead; the bangs still emphasize the untouched real estate of her very blue eyes. Her face tuck is so tight that when she smiles, her toes curl up. Even as she sails through late middle age, her choice of boyfriends remains curly-haired and smiley young men who don't mind being taken care of.

"What do you think of . . . ?" The problem of immigration, the problem of preschool education, the problem of raising money for the San Francisco Art Institute, the problem of the excess of fashion shows for good causes. She needs a comment from the young man.

"It's fabulous how you're so involved, Donna," he had better say. "I've never met anybody with your, well, how to put it — range of concerns? The whole spectrum?"

"I'm a spiritual person," she admits. More into spirituality than generosity, nurturing is not really her thing, but an estate with monthly disbursements can serve just as well for the smiley, curly-haired young men.

2

A Night Scavenger

Tolstoy's notorious verdict was that happy families are all alike, but every unhappy family is unhappy in its own way. Every divorce is supposed to be unhappy, and usually succeeds in this, despite the efforts of tender couples to make theirs one of the miracle happy ones. A gracious and cooperative divorce can be worse because the uncauterized wound continues to bleed. Hatred might allow the wound to be closed under a scar that can be lived with.

Mine was a tender and friendly divorce. Overwhelmed by three babies in diapers, a daughter and twin sons, my wife held herself together until one evening when she marched back and forth across our living room — I was lying on the floor with a child on my chest, playing an airplane game — and announced that she had to divorce something, life was too complicated, she felt like a prisoner. Since she couldn't divorce her children, she would divorce her husband. It was a time of feminist eruption, especially in San Francisco. One of our friends confided that her husband didn't know their two children weren't his by birth; he loved them; what he didn't know didn't hurt him, right?

For many men, it was a miserable time. I was one of those. We developed procedures of caution and affability.

On a sunny late afternoon I arrived, as usual, to visit our sons, Ari and Ethan, and Nina, our daughter. I was wearing a jacket and tie because I was then going on to a consular reception for a visiting writer. As I left, Melissa asked, "What's happening?" I told her. She hesitated a moment, then said, "Would you like my company?"

Of course I would. "Do you want to go?"

"I've got a babysitter coming. What should I wear?"

"Fine, good, what you've got on — you always dress right."

As usual, when she swept shy and seductive glances over me during these visits, or unshy and seductive gestures, inviting me to stay for dinner, stay for the night, I thought once again, Oh, it's all been a mistake, our marriage is not over. On these occasions, I would leave in the middle of the night, driving back to my flat at one or two in the morning, not sure what was going on and fearing to confuse our children if they woke up to find Daddy back again for breakfast. I was confused enough for all concerned. "Fine, good, sure, I said that already."

She put her hand to her mouth. "Oh, dear. Just a sec while I call" — she named her new lover — "and head him off before he leaves Marin."

She had to break a date with her lover in order to spend an evening with her husband? In a black rage the words burst out: "Never mind! Don't! Just don't!" There was a nightmare creature inhabiting the body of the one who loved his wife, loved his children, and couldn't comprehend the chaos invading his world. It was a despairing and hate-filled creature.

30

"Never mind, don't, see you tomorrow," and I fled to my battered Fiat with its ragged canvas sunroof. The years, the children, and the imprint still on my flesh from the times we had walked together in the San Francisco dusk, or listened in the dark to the wail of Bob Dylan, or danced, picnicked, or confided as lovers do, had all come to this — a time when she decided to break a date with a lover in order to join her husband.

She ran alongside the Fiat as I started to drive away. She said: "I just want you to know I'd rather be with you than with him."

Then why? I refused to understand, three children didn't understand, and this intelligent, clear-eyed woman didn't understand, either, but felt an imperative that superseded understanding. It was the mid-seventies, women were trying to puzzle out their lives, and for some it was a great liberating adventure. Some men were following on this uncharted path. Others were learning both to whine and that whining did no good. *Why*, I whined, and drove to the consular reception. Since I was alone in my emergency "pre-owned" Fiat, the question *why?* found no one in the vicinity to answer it, no one to point out the necessary: Hey, Buster, you're whining — not very useful.

My nose was pointed toward an uncertain future; my steering wheel was at risk due to episodes of abrupt inattention. I wasn't a good driver after those late-night secret assignations with my wife. They left me confused. Husbands shouldn't be heading home under the glare of streetlamps at three A.M. or in the first glimmer of dawn — and where was home, anyway? I had bought a mechanically deficient used Fiat; an accident would solve no problems. Suicide was frequently on offer. I had the task of arguing myself away from a stupid end. In Plato, Aristotle, Spinoza, John Donne, and my children I was able to find reasons for not creating an accident, children being the most compelling ones.

Self-pity is about as useful as jealousy; even Peeping Tomism is more productive. This should not be construed as a recommendation to climb a tree and spy on the beloved through her, formerly our, bedroom window. Instead, I took other measures, such as grinding my teeth and wandering.

In Buena Vista Park, I met a young woman whom I noticed because (a) she was a pretty frowner with close-knit eyebrows and (b) she was sitting on a bench with her book reading the same page over and over. I offered to help her interpret if it was French, but it turned out to be *Finnegans Wake*. I couldn't speed up the young woman's deciphering of James Joyce's masterpiece, but after some expert conversation about Giambattista Vico (1668–1744), the "eternal return," the relevance of the River Liffey in Irish mythology — the usual stuff everyone talks about in Buena Vista Park when they're not throwing Frisbees — it developed that the young woman was willing to continue the discussion by paying me a visit after I put my sons to sleep on their futons in my apartment. It further developed that she slipped into the empty side of my bed.

Unfortunately, she didn't leave in the middle of the night. Ari, when he came running in the morning in his footie Charlie Brown pajamas to jump into bed with me as usual, stopped suddenly when he noticed the stranger. He stared a moment and then turned and ran back to his futon.

It was a confusing time for everyone. Folks were restless. Later that day, the pretty Joyce scholar with close-knit eyebrows when she frowned left me a frowning poem, which I interpreted as "Good-bye forever." This was the correct interpretation.

In San Francisco, the weather seldom requires a decision about opening or shutting the window — it's always okay out there. My inner weather was not okay. Born in the Midwest, where big boys don't cry, I rediscovered tears. Ethan, who is now a musician, composed his first song at age four, with a chorus that went, "Dumb daddy dumb, dumb daddy dumb." Later he offered me a contribution to the country western genre: "My baby done left me, / So I went downstairs and ate some fried chicken."

A child nails his parents' conditions, no matter how well parents think they are concealing them. Coolly and lovingly, sometimes more one than the other, a child makes his own judgments.

I tried to drive carefully. My effort was not successful. Suffering a drastic sudden impulse to telephone my wife, I parked near a pay phone on a steep San Francisco hill. ("And another thing I wanted to say . . .") I neglected to pull the hand brake and curb the wheels. The Fiat started to roll, me frantically chasing it. A pair of compassionate gay men saw what was happening and drove their automobile in front of mine to block the imminent catastrophe at an intersection. When I visited them later with money and flowers, they blushed modestly, and one said, "Always glad to be of service, anytime." I promised better motoring care in the future.

I was looking not to find my way, but to find a way to look for it that kept me alive; that is, kept me awake and not a danger to others. Maybe I could learn to enjoy my misery because it was another approach to the interesting world out there.

I curbed my wheels on hills. I paid attention. In a time of bad fortune, I reminded myself of my good fortune in life.

Back in the beatnik flat above North Beach where I had lived before Melissa and I met, unable to sleep, I followed my own course of insomnia treatment — giving up sleeping. San Francisco permits year-round night wandering without galoshes or an overcoat even if the head was abjectly lowered and the shoulders hunched until I reminded myself: *Raise head. Unhunch shoulders. You're not dead yet.* The four directions were each different: north to the Bay, Aquatic Park, and Fisherman's Wharf with its sea smells mixed with decaying crab and fish head pungencies, awaiting scavengers, attended by furtive rats but no tourists at three in the morning; south toward Nob Hill and chic hotels, especially the Fairmont with its all-night brasserie, welcoming jet-lagged tourists along with pimps and their girls reaping the rewards of after-work Rest & Recreation (eggs, pancakes, a kind word or two, plus Mission Control debriefing); east into North Beach, where a few drunks might still be stumbling among the homeless in doorways, shooting up if they were lucky enough to cop their drugs; west toward Polk, formerly the gay main street, now replaced by Castro, but still housing a few traditional bars, such as the White Swallow.

Tonight I chose Polk. There would be company, runaways selling drugs or themselves, gray wolves cruising for boys or drugs, a depressed midway of night scavengers prowling in the eerie glow of neon and fog-shrouded streetlamps. Besides the men's shop called The Gray Wolf, servicing aging Polk Street trollers, and the White Swallow bar, Hard On

Leathers, and Travel Agency for Trips, there was a selection of twenty-four-hour adult bookstores catering to every marketable specialty. Transvestites and transsexuals waited for something to happen. At the intersection of Polk and Geary, female vigilantes from the Jewish Lesbian Gang watched over the traffic, looking for roaming homophobes to beat up. After a stroll among nature and nurture, I planned to take breakfast at the all-night, sometimes most-of-the-night, diner at Polk and Pine. It was designed to resemble a car on a train crossing great, true hearted America and issuing lonely hooting calls over the plains. But then again, I wasn't sure about many things, including where to have breakfast.

Many of the men in doorways with a red glow on their faces, ardently inhaling whatever they were smoking, stood with the lowered head and hunched shoulders I had forbidden for myself. They may have thought they looked like James Dean, but they didn't. As I went by, a young man moved forward from under the canopy of a spiritual bookstore, asking, "So how are you this evening?"

I didn't correct him. Four A.M. is no longer evening. It should be called "night." He wasn't looking for linguistic pedantry, and I wasn't looking for what he was offering; I was looking for fresh-squeezed orange juice. At that time on Polk in San Francisco, unlike at four A.M. in my home town of Cleveland, a diner stood open nearby for fresh-squeezed orange juice, coffee, doughnuts, and muffins, and behind the counter, her legs wide, a heavy-lidded Cantonese woman waited with tongs for muffin-lifting and a baseball bat for head-bashing. She was seriously balding and had dyed her scalp to match her shopping-bag-pink hair. I sipped juice, warmed my hands on a mug of coffee, took pleasure in my moroseness. Alcohol-comedown beveraging was in progress at a table where another night wanderer muttered at the spillage from his own or a previous customer's mug. Despite our gray-flecked beards and discontented faces, there were significant differences between us. His coffee was black, mine had milk in it. The diner glowed: tiles, formica, mirrors, flickering fluorescent tubes, a different version of great, true-hearted America. Most of the other men — there were no women customers — were on stools at the counter with U.S. currency peeking out of their shirt pockets (drugs on offer) or red bandannas hanging from the back pockets of jeans (sex on offer, individual specialty signaled by whether it was the left or right pocket that displayed the bandanna.)

The red-bandanna guys thought I was a gray wolf, but I was merely an insomniac night wanderer. The U.S. currency guys must have thought I was a busted alkie because I showed no life. Sipping juice, sipping coffee, giving up on sleep, waiting for dawn, I didn't know what I was. This was mildly consoling. At least I was ready for alternatives.

Elsewhere, my children were asleep and my wife was cuddled asleep or awake in a way my entire body remembered with a shiver. With someone not the father of her children. Not me. So how was I this evening? Not great.

One persistent young man, a double-threat conglomerate, both a red bandanna hanging from the left back pocket of his jeans and money peeking from his snap-button shirt pocket, smiled and moved closer. An unsnapped pink button flashed a glimpse of chest; his eyes crinkled like a Marlboro cowboy's; he knew how to jump-start a friendship. "Howdy, dude," he said, "so don't you deserve someone to be an excellent pal this evening?"

No, thanks; orange juice and coffee were just fine.

Stoked by distraction and memories, also half a bran muffin, and having walked the length of the street, I noticed that the sky was beginning to brighten. Pigeons were following their nighttime snacks with early-morning breakfast on pizza rinds left at curbs, and now the dawn pink shimmered in the fog and two scavenger trucks were grinding at the intersection and my legs were tired. The rats scurrying underfoot didn't fear me; they scurried only because they were in a hurry to get to the pizza, takeout chow mein, and with luck, a baby pigeon, before their colleagues buried their own snouts in grease or feathers. There was enough for all, but rats don't stop to think with generosity. This Styrofoam container right here might spill out the last noodles on earth.

I climbed the hill toward my apartment. I might be able to sleep. Later in the day, I wanted to be awake, lively, and emanating cheer-ismo for the children in their mother's house.

Night again, another night, unavoidable, very tired, breathing shallowly but making the rational choice — go to bed. I dropped into sleep, followed by a stomach-churning dream, which of course led to the abrupt end of sleep. I sat up with a start. The nightmare I could not abide was the one where the woman who had taken my arm with love, filled my arms with warmth, was telling me that our two sons and daughter were not my children. In real life she didn't tell me this, but I heard her saying it in a nightmare and leapt awake, nauseated, sobbing. It wasn't so, I knew it wasn't so, and yet the nightmare declared it to be so. We had slept in each other's arms, seized each other on Mount Tamalpais, laughing and sliding on weeds and fallen eucalyptus leaves, devouring each other. I had swaggered around, declaring her a statistical miracle. So how could our history be erased? If it was — the logic of nightmare — these children who resembled us both, ideal mixtures of Ashkenazic Jew and Anglo-Scottish WASP, were . . . But of course this was only a nightmare, as I knew, of course I knew, and was attacked by it anyway.

It was still another night filled with the sleep devils. Better to wake and walk. The city offered another night of gloom for my enjoyment.

This time it needed to end with breakfast at the all-night brasserie in the Fairmont Hotel. I was hungry for an omelet, blueberry pancakes, or corned beef hash, like a business traveler from Japan or Germany. The time-zone victims might look less haggard and red-eyed than the fellow who lived less than ten blocks away. Divorce is not the moral equivalent of jet lag, but like jet lag, this pain doesn't last forever, unless it does. I assumed I could outlast my misery and nightmares if they were serving fresh blueberry pancakes.

I walked down Russian Hill and up the slope of Nob Hill, passing a *New York Times* box, and decided to use my quarters here. It was dark and cold, a winter fog hanging heavy. I inserted my coins, opened the box. A tall man with a little goatee stepped out of the darkness, opened a briefcase, showed me a pistol, and said politely, "Put your wallet in here, sir." Another man, short and broad, stood behind him.

What went through my mind was: Odd that he didn't hold the pistol in his hand. What followed was: If I let go of the newspaper box, I'll forfeit my quarters. What followed — no, the three thoughts were simultaneous — was: *Run.*

I grabbed *The New York Times* and took off without warmup at a speed that had once snapped my Achilles tendon. This time the only damage was an insult from the two polite robbers: "Asshole!"

My muggers seemed to be too lazy to chase me. A few blocks away, I flagged down a police car. I was sure I would recognize the robbers. The cops put me in the car, and we toured the neighborhood. No luck. Later, the cops brought a sheet with photos of black and brown men: four with goatees, four without and short. I was sure I would pick out the right guys. I couldn't. No smart witnessing. The cops told me the "Mutt and Jeff bandits" had, an hour before our meeting, broken the arm of a stockbroker headed for his office. Brokerage firms need to prepare for the New York opening. Due to the time change, they are early risers, walking down Telegraph, Russian, and Nob hills like spirits of the night in business suits. My two would-be muggers were known as Mutt and Jeff because one was tall and the other short. Perhaps they didn't chase me because they were tired after beating up a broker, stripping off his clothes. Could I please, the cops asked, help them out?

I still couldn't choose among the photos. "I pride myself on my powers of observation," I muttered.

"So try again. Make a stab."

"The short one had an ass as big as all outdoors."

"Ha-ha," said the black cop with no humor at all except the irritated kind. "You're not trying."

I tried again. I failed. The two policemen who crowded my flat the next day were as disappointed in me as the muggers had been. Not only had I failed to keep my marriage going in a time when many failed, but also I failed to identify the Mutt and Jeff who interrupted my quest for healing all-night blueberry pancakes.

The night of my mugging was a night without rest, but there will always be more, won't there? I missed my dreams of loss; metabolism took over. With sunlight, the miracle of alertness returned when I played softball with my children in the schoolyard across the street from their mother's house. "Just pitch! And don't throw the bat!"

So regular it seemed endless was the supply of nights. I awakened from the memory dream of holding my wife in my arms during a time when all the world, and especially Bob Dylan, The Band, Joan Baez, and the taste of love, were young. Surely they were, maybe I wasn't, but seeming had been sufficient unto that day. On still another night, I arose from my bed and headed for the brasserie at the Fairmont for those delayed blueberry . . . well, to change my luck, maybe something else.

I passed *The New York Times* box at Clay and Taylor and wondered if Mutt and Jeff had ever been caught. There was dew on the box; there was a fresh stack of papers; but I decided not to dilute the pleasure of my oncoming pancake treats with a bath in world disasters. After making my way through the ornate, glowing, dimmed lobby, clerks and security guards sleepily on duty, I found company in the brasserie, a little group of German travelers applying beer to their jet lag, and the usual pimps with their girls enjoying R&R after an evening's work well or at least adequately done. Like them, I was a night scavenger.

But I could still surprise myself. "I'll have the French toast and a pot of coffee."

"Good choice," murmured the waiter, dutiful, but tired of saying the same thing to everyone. Little did he know that my blueberry pancake plan had gone astray.

"And the orange juice, is it fresh?" Todd (according to his badge) didn't good-choice me, so I wouldn't know if he had heard until the juice arrived or didn't.

The girl at the next table was pale and made paler by the slash of lipstick across her mouth. She was gazing beseechingly, worshipfully, at the sharp dude with the rings and the cowboy hat who was turning his high beams on her as if she were a favorite child, which at this moment she was. His other girls were still out somewhere, or had not lived up to quota, or possibly they had done everything right but this member of the stable, in her rotation, was due for an elegant predawn dining experience. The dude noticed my noticing him. "Hey," he inquired, "what the fuck you lookin' at?"

"Your hat. I like the hat."

He turned his high beams on me. We were instant buddies. "Stetson, man, with the buffalo-fuzz trim, on my trip to Dallas. Tole them what I wanted at the Cowboy Rancho Shop-pe — write down that name."

I could understand how he made friends with lost girls since he was already making friends with a lost middle-aged man.

Another thought occurred to him. "You lookin' for anythin', big guy?"

"Naw," I confessed falsely, "just breakfast. But Stetson, I'll remember that."

"You do." Then he turned and patted the wrist of the Sharon or Debbie or Julie-Mae from the Greyhound station. She blushed, Todd arrived, she bent, blushing, to her . . . Good Lord! My blueberry pancakes! We scavengers of the night were all in this together, it seemed. And when I had expected a staredown, a threat, something ominous after meeting the eyes of my neighboring fellow breakfaster, he gave me nothing but a fraternal offer of haberdashery info.

I lingered over my coffee. There wouldn't be frost outside, this was San Francisco, but there would be a humid, damp San Francisco predawn chill. Todd, the good-choice waitperson, returned with his silver pot and his next dialogue staple: "Another splash?" I nodded. He refilled my cup.

Wise good choice because then another night-world distraction from marital blues came to fill the hour. There was a loud scraping of chair. Abruptly it seemed as if the Fairmont lights flickered and dimmed without a generator picking up the slack. A wrathful chair scraped, then another chair, and a table lifted and thumped down; the scattered night diners drew away, except for those who drew closer to the excitement. The Germans were alert and happy. *Gott im himmel*, here was fun and turmoil that was actual, not on television. The outcall girl had found her inner vixen. The slash of lipstick looked like a wound, but her eyes were undaunted behind mascara hanging loosely from her lashes. She found her inner vixen's oratorical skills, too. "Fucker!" she screamed, and elaborated, made more precise: "*Mother*fucker!"

Then the innocent child hooker metamorphosed into an avenging child hooker, flinging her plateload of sliced syrupy blueberry pancakes at her protector. Perhaps out of respect, not yet an entire all-out battling child hooker, she held back the plate itself, at least pending further developments, only spattering blueberries and syrup on the no longer smiling pimp's Stetson. "My hat!" he howled.

He should have removed it for early A.M. dining. He didn't take the insult to self and haberdashery well. He reached across and grabbed his ward's hair, yanking her down to the floor in front of his splayed legs, but by this time rapid-reaction-force Fairmont security guards were on him, two of them, grabbing him by the arms, shoulders, perhaps even an ear — it happened so fast — while he roared, "Racists!"

One of them was laughing while definitely pulling him by the ear and the other frisked him, looking for gun, knife, or razor, and the ear guy was saying, "I'm blacker'n you, asshole, no fighting, you're eighty-sixed from the Fairmont Hotel." Disgustedly he emptied the man's pockets of a couple of glassine envelopes. "Get the fuck out, no shit, or you're in worse trouble, brother."

This was a reasonable hair-pulling pimp with a damaged Stetson. He decided to go quietly, which was best under present glassine-envelope circumstances. Meekly the girl followed, as he knew she would, all passion spent. Her storm passed. Neither she nor her escort wanted any serious interruption of their relationship. The Germans at the next table were saying things in German to each other, and although I didn't know German and therefore couldn't read German lips, it seemed to be on the order of, "We always knew San Francisco was a party town."

As I passed the table of delighted Germans, who were enjoying the tried-and-true beer, steak, and eggs remedy for jet lag, a strong scent of ketchup and cigar smoke followed me. Salt, tomatoes, illegal Cuban Upmanns, all sorting themselves out in my own alert, amply caffeined state. The brief scuffle meant nothing, yet must have meant something. The security guards kept the glassine envelopes as a nice perk.

On the walk home, lifted by social events, breathing deeply of the fresh-air scent of early-morning, red-streaked skies, I passed a *San Francisco Chronicle* box next to the *New York Times* box where, on another occasion, I had declined the offer to be mugged. The one-star edition displayed a boxed headline with a black outline at the top of the front page: ZERO MOSTEL, ACTOR, DIES.

I remembered watching the play by Ionesco in which Zero's immense but agile body miraculously seemed to transform itself into a snorting rhinoceros, bristling with tusks. In the audience Melissa and I hugged each other to stop choking with laughter, the Heimlich maneuver of lovers sharing joy. The news made me feel as if I had wrapped my hand around broken glass. Having given so much pleasure, Zero Mostel now ruined the night, interrupted mere depression with grief.

At my apartment, putting on an LP but turning the speaker volume down so as not to wake the neighbors, I played a side by John Fahey, known as "Blind Joe Death," the guitar bard of underground beatnik Berkeley from the time when a woman came along to make me laugh and Zero Mostel came to make us laugh together.

3

Lakewood, Ohio, 1930s

A big boy named Jack lived in the house next door. In our house, I was a littler boy and my brother, Sid, was the even littler one who liked to tag along with me. Although the houses stood side by side in Lakewood, Ohio, only a driveway between them, Jack never played with us. Occasionally when we passed on the sidewalk, Sid and I dawdling our way home from Taft Elementary and Jack from the parochial school a few blocks away, he would shout, "Chrith Killerth!" with a spray of saliva flying from his mouth.

I asked Mother what he was saying.

"He'll grow out of it," she explained, exercising her habit of answering the question she preferred to answer, rather than the one asked. Sid looked at me, trusting me to give him an interpretation, but I didn't have one. Did she mean he would grow out of his lisp or his accusation? I knew it was an accusation because of the shrillness of his voice, the specks of foam at his lips. When he whispered, if we happened to pass close to him, Sid wanting to take my hand but not daring to, it was no more agreeable.

Jack's mother seemed to have no husband; Jack's father was invisible. There was a glassed-in perch on the roof of the

45

McDonald house, and sometimes Mrs. McDonald, whom we took to calling the Old Crab, stared at our house even if our shades were pulled down. More often, she peered out toward Lake Erie, a few blocks away, beyond the streetcar line on Clifton Boulevard, which led into Cleveland. Since I didn't ask, Mother told me what she was looking for — her husband. He was a captain on a ship carrying iron ore and may have gotten off in Duluth. On Hathaway Avenue it was known that he had been gone for many years.

At age seven or eight, in bed with the measles, feverish and itching, I was asleep one late afternoon when an open can of sardines came flying through the window. Jack had thrown it from the driveway alongside. Mother picked up the jagged can and cleaned up the mess of oil and fish, but the pungent stink of sardines lingered, sickeningly, until she finally took Clorox to the stains on the floor. I pointed out the streaks of bleach. She said "*Meshuganeh*," and of course I didn't know if she meant me or the McDonalds, mother and son. She didn't explain and didn't bother to add an irrelevant comment, either. Crazy was in the air.

Extreme remedies were required to wipe away the Christ-killer smells. Our neighbors' battle against those who not only crucified their Savior but also mowed their lawn on the sabbath was unrelenting. Dad liked to garden on his day free of work in the Gold Bros. store; Officer Cecil wearily paid us another visit, explaining, "There's been a complaint . . ." From a pulled curtain, Mrs. McDonald's eyes peered out at the black-and-white police car at the curb. Politely, Officer Cecil stayed for one of Mother's oatmeal-raisin cookies and a cup of Nestlé's instant coffee because he knew the Old Crab was watching, hoping to see the sabbathdesecrater dragged off to jail. Dad gave Officer Cecil a Christmas basket of fruit every year, but the policeman had sworn to do his duty. He saw that Sid was frightened by his uniform. He said, "Hi, sonny," and patted his head. Since I wasn't frightened but curious, he treated me to a manly nod. Sitting down at the kitchen table to his cookie and coffee, he said, "Mr. Gold, I'm sorry, your truck starts up pretty noisy, maybe a tune-up . . . Mr. Gold, I'm sorry, if you could ask the kids not to run around so much in the backyard . . . Mr. Gold, about your lawn, you keep a nice lawn, but I'm sorry . . ."

The Lake Erie boat captain never came home. Mrs. McDonald kept watch over us nearby more than she studied the lake four blocks away. My brother and I were growing up and so was Jack McDonald, forever a few years ahead of us. Occasionally he still bounced a tennis ball against our house at naptimes, but Sid and I stopped needing afternoon naps. The sardines were only a one-time suggestion from his mom. Sid and I got used to walking past the McDonald house without fear, although we averted our eyes and Sid moved closer to me. We didn't stop to stare and satisfy our curiosity about the mysterious mother and son.

Once Dad remarked, "I never heard about no ore boat sank. Wintertime they close down the lake anyways. It's Siberia out there." He made these weather observations to the world in general, expecting no reply, and then retreated into his chair to read *Der Tag* (*The Day*), a newspaper he received by mail from New York. "Ain't coming home, smart guy, that's all," he grumbled.

I tried to puzzle things out from Dad's grumbles, Mother's impatience, Officer Cecil's visits, the glaring eyes of

Mrs. McDonald behind curtains pulled aside, the occasional rhythmic bounce of an old tennis ball against the side of our house. Putting all the evidence together, I came to understand that our family was the only one on Hathaway Avenue that didn't accept Jesus, we rejected Him, and as Father Coughlin advised, the money-changers needed to be driven from the temple; also the Sunday mowers from their lawns. Also, early-morning truck-starters with slow ignitions in cold weather should go back where they came from.

The Black Legion, night riders out of Jackson, Michigan, was organizing its stalwart paranoids against race pollution. The white hood of the Kluxers was a Southern thing, below the class level of the sophisticates of Jackson, Grass Lake, and certain enclaves of outer Detroit. The Silver Shirts, led by William Dudley Pelley, wore a different color from the Nazi brown or Legion black because they were fighting the war on an all-American front. The German-American Bund marched in Cleveland, Milwaukee, and New York, and supported student exchange programs for American and German kids. ("I didn't see any persecution of Jews," one returning scholar reported to our school assembly. "Of course, I didn't see any Jews, either." There was laughter. There were only a couple of Jewish families in Lakewood, but everyone knew who they were.)

From the Shrine of the Little Flower in Royal Oak, Michigan, Father Coughlin broadcast his anathemas in a resonant tenor, which echoed from most of the radios up and down Hathaway Avenue on Sunday mornings.

"Mother," I asked, "what's a shrine?"

"Who shrine? What *farkokteh* shrine?"

"Shrine of the Little Flower."

"Don't you have better things than why are you asking dumb questions? So are you ready for your lesson tomorrow, five prompt? I bought the piano, I pay her even if you don't learn nothing. If you don't practice, I'm gonna . . ." She paused, stymied for only a moment. When I didn't empty my plate, she reminded me of the starving Armenians who would be happy for it. But I knew there was no danger of sending the upright piano to any starving Armenians. "I'm gonna give it to Officer Cecil for his kid, plays good already."

From behind his copy of *Der Tag*, Dad said, "Irving in the store thinks that big mouth Father Cofflin makes sense. That's why Irving is nothing but my bookkeeper I don't fire because I'm sorry for a dummy and his wife."

Mother made a further contribution to family enlightenment. "Sam, sometimes your son is also a dummy. He left his glass of citrus on the table, didn't even drink it, for me to not let it go to waste. Don't he know these are hard times?"

I knew, but wasn't telling.

"He has problems," Mother concluded, dwindling but doing a responsible parent's best to improve her eldest son's behavior in every way, from piano playing to not wasting. I was supposed to play "The Harmonious Blacksmith" at the recital, but was I ready? No.

I picked up my copies of the Silver Shirt newspaper from the bundle regularly dropped at the entrance to Taft School. It didn't answer my curiosity about money-changers in the Shrine of the Little Father, but it informed me that President Roosevelt's real name was Rosenfelt. Around that time, Richard, my best friend since kindergarten — everyone has a best friend at that age — explained that I couldn't be invited to his birthday parties anymore because his mother thought some of the other mothers, those of girls, wouldn't let their daughters attend. Richard was still my best friend for stamp collecting, street baseball, and book reading. For his birthday, I gave him a copy of *Ted Scott Across the Frozen North*, latest in the Ted Scott, Intrepid Flyer, series we both collected.

It was an interesting time to be the only family of our sort in the neighborhood, our sort being money-changers and race polluters, with cloven hooves and horns cunningly hidden in our hair. The suddenly altering girls, finding strange growths on their own bodies with no warning from their mothers, could easily imagine, even if they couldn't see, the horns concealed in the pompadour I adopted from Dad. One of the girls, adventurous red-haired Donna, asked me to take off my left shoe so she could check my hoof. I refused, but she gave me a quick kiss on the cheek anyway, promising more when I grew up. Sex was ominous, Jews were ominous; since the first excited interest, so did the second. But it was too soon for me to think of this as an advantage.

Something about the situation also interested the older boy next door. One afternoon, Mother and Dad at work in the store, as they usually were, Jack McDonald suddenly appeared at our front door, calling my name. I had just finished pouring glasses of milk for Sid and me; I'd opened a box of graham crackers. Jack was saying, "Hey! In there! Hey, how the heck are you?"

"Okay," I said cautiously.

"Wanna see my house? Both of you?" He was wearing a brown corduroy lumberjacket and corduroy pants. His hands were in his pockets. His house was a mysterious and menacing presence, dark, the shades pulled down, the curtains drawn. Mother instructed us, "Don't look back," when the Old Crab's face peeked at us from behind a curtain, searching out our sins. "Why not?" I asked, and Mother answered: "Hurt your eyes, dummy. Don't you have something better? Go practice, I wanna hear that Handel tune perfect."

After so many years, of course I wanted to see inside Jack's house. He stood there, legs spread, meatily smiling. "Come on. Sid, you can come, too. Mom took the streetcar to Cleveland, there's a sale at Higbee's. Won't be home till supper, earliest."

It was amazing that the Old Crab went shopping like normal human mothers. Sid was hanging at my heels, as usual. "Come on," I commanded.

As Jack moved upstairs, the Gold brothers behind him, his buttocks in brown corduroy wobbled a bit. He was thick and growing thicker. Sid and I were still children. The McDonald living room smelled of being closed off, with lace doilies on tables, scattered photographs of the absent ore boat captain, some with deckled edges, a giant metal cigarette-lighting machine with an open carton of Lucky Strikes alongside, and a heart-shaped twisted-silver frame containing a portrait of the Old Crab as a pretty young woman with bobbed hair wearing a wedding dress. Her groom stared gloomily into the camera.

Jack slid the coffee table off to the side, leaving a wide expanse of carpet. "How about a rassle?" he asked. "Show you some a my special moves."

I was still thinking about the offer when he grabbed me around the neck. I struggled, thought of kicking, but worried that the Old Crab would find out I had kicked her son and would call Officer Cecil and then what trouble I'd be in. We fell to the floor, my nose buried in gritty carpet. I yelled, "Lemme go!" very loudly, "lemme go, lemme go!"

Wrestling with Jack McDonald was no fun — the carpet burn, the sweat off his thick body, the tightness of his arm. But maybe wrestlers were supposed to grab and squeeze and hold and drive someone's nose into the floor.

He let me up. Red-faced but smiling, his buckteeth outgoing and friendly, he said to Sid, "Okay, your turn. I'll teach you the great moves. I got moves you can't learn from those dummies at Taft." He loomed over us. "I got expert-tiss."

My face must have revealed that we hadn't heard this word before, not even on the Fred Allen show, which brought big words to my radio experience.

"Expert-tease," he explained.

Sid, smaller than I was, much smaller than Jack, didn't know what to do. He stood there waiting, his short pants hanging below his knees. He didn't know what was supposed to happen next, while I pretended, since I was nearly two years older than my brother, that this *rassling* was nothing new in my sophisticated life. We could learn some expert-tiss.

"Come on, I'm ready," Jack said. Sid put up his arms. "On your mark, get set —" With a distant smile on his face, still blotched red after his exertions with me, Jack just stepped into Sid, pinning his arms to his sides, and they fell together to the carpet. Had I looked as helpless as Sid did? They rolled on the floor, Jack grunting, "Okay, okay, rassle with me."

Then he was on top of my little brother, pressing hard. "Let me go," Sid gasped. I cried out, "Hey! That's enough! Let him go!"

A sudden smell like wet firecrackers arose in the closed

room. I grabbed Jack's shoulders, trying to pull him off, but I didn't need to pull — he just fell off to the side and lay there, eyes shut but still grinning. The wet firecracker smell was sour; sweat, smoldering ashes, and Jack McDonald stretched out on the floor with a meaty goofy grin.

"Come on, Sid, we're going," I said.

Neither of us spoke of the wrestling to our mother or anyone, not even to each other, and although it sometimes came to mind on the sidewalk in front of the McDonald house, I never asked Sid if he remembered it. When we glimpsed Jack, he never beckoned to us, never again invited us into his house, but also never again called us Christ-killers. We avoided looking at him.

In years that followed, I realized that my grumbling father probably was right. There was no news in *Der Tag* or the Cleveland *Plain Dealer* of the tragic sinking of a Lake Erie ore carrier bound for Duluth. I too became an inspector of texts. When my hormones flooded with the adolescent growth spurt, no doubt similar to the parochial school hormones of Jack McDonald, I understood that Lilith, a siren with long silky lashes, had sung her ancient songs to Jack's father and had drawn Captain McDonald to dash his ship against the rocks of adultery, perhaps as nearby as Sandusky. I was learning about life from books. Lilith steals the strength of men's loins while they sleep. The Old Crab couldn't compete with the cursed Hebrew first bride of Adam, fiery Lilith, who was so skilled at forcing pleasure upon the Captain. It was a bewilderment she also brought to me, awakening me regularly to dizzy crashings like those which marooned the Captain in Sandusky, Toledo, or perhaps ashore at the distant port of Duluth in fabled, glamorous Minnesota. Lilith promised him the secret of unendurable pleasure indefinitely prolonged. He gave it a try. Captain McDonald, husband and father, never returned to Lakewood, Ohio.

The confusion of the times succeeded in confusing me despite my avid reading. The smell of my father's Sunday-mown grass when Officer Cecil came to our door, wearily suggesting, "Mr. Gold, I'm sorry, but you should do this maybe how about some other day?" The smell of the closed house next door. The smell of wet firecrackers, the smell of an open can of sardines smearing the floor of my bedroom. The smell of Lakewood, Ohio, in the 1930s.

But in years that followed, I came to bless Jack McDonald as we passed silently on the sidewalk. Wonderment and gratitude flowed over me because he had taught me something it had been time for me to learn, that part of my job in life was to protect my brother. Of course I often failed at this, as brothers often do.

4

A Selfish Story

"Daddy, were you in World War One or Two?" my daughter Ann asked me. At about the same time, a woman whom I considered as grown-up as myself told me that she remembered my war because she remembered the boots her father wore while washing the car. She was an infant on an Army post. And yet, for those who enlisted near our eighteenth birthdays in the early forties, the war is still immediate, our youth may be gone but not disappeared, even if time and history have rolled over us.

In 1942, I embraced New York City. I had spent a year wandering on the road, hitchhiking, living through a fantasy of rebellion from Cleveland, part of it in the flops of the Bowery and Bleecker Street, but now I washed and scrubbed myself, turned seventeen and a half, and entered Columbia College. Morningside Heights was as far from my scrounging boy hobo days as any place could be; Irwin Edman, Lionel Trilling, and Mark Van Doren replaced the gamblers and shills on Key Largo, the enraged, oversteamed chefs in restaurant kitchens all up and down the eastern seaboard, the losers, wildballs, and predators of the risky America I had pursued.

Having so much eccentric fun made me earnest. I grew toward being an adjusted misfit.

The experience of college structure was brief. We freshmen, turning eighteen, believed we might finish our first year before going to war. During the autumn of 1942, the black winter, reluctant spring, we read Homer and Thucydides, piled into Humanities and Contemporary Civilization, and felt up the Barnard girls near the spiked metal fence on Broadway. We discussed our future silver wings, our marksmen's medals, our citations and press dispatches to come. We had no imagination for death, for our own inevitable future deaths, the death of everyone, and for the complicating fact that a certain proportion of these readers of bloody Homer and the wrath of Achilles would be dead early, very soon now, before the end of the war.

The normal static of late boyhood interferes with the process of growing up, imagining mortality. Knowledge comes at moments in the flux and flow; a serious illness; the death of a parent. Sometimes even education can educate. By pure good fortune, one of these moments occurred during a lazy late-winter afternoon in Hamilton Hall; the steam heat was boiling, there was a smell of chalk in the air, a seminar on "Lucretius and Time" was occupying a group of solemn freshmen and our teacher, O. J. Campbell, a distinguished scholar of Shakespeare. Until this afternoon, I had not formed any close friendships at school, although I admired the mad Cuban of Hartley Hall, who ran naked up and down the corridors, and a boy with a Maine accent who wanted to be either a missionary in Africa or a dean at Bowdoin, and an irritable freshman from White Plains who felt misused because he was merely adopted into a rich family, not born to it. Jack Kerouac was on the football team, a popular jock. Having spent a year on the road, I felt cut off from him and the other middle-class youngsters making their way on squads and in clubs. I didn't even write for *Jester*, the college humor magazine, or the *Spectator*. I was a secret poet and journal keeper.

On that sleepy, still afternoon in Hamilton Hall, a crucial discovery was opened to me, and with it, I also made my first close college friend. Professor Campbell, looking out over the dozen of us slouched around a table, talking about time and time's end, life and mortality, suddenly remarked to this solemn crew, "I was dead once, but I came back. I was dead and I remember it." He had had a heart attack; he had gone under; then he had returned. "I was dead. I still remember." The words were ordinary, but in the act of uttering them, he suddenly forgot to speak. He put his head down and remembered. Thick gray eyebrows, a heavy, handsome old head. A look of withdrawal, a look of the deepest seriousness possessed him. There was an uneasy silence in the room.

Ahead of my first risk in the war, ahead of my first dangerous illness, ahead of the first death of someone close to me, I had a premonition of what death might mean, beyond the drama of grief and mourning. My own heart stopped. There was the excitement of discovery and a terrible loneliness.

At that moment, and perhaps just as Professor Campbell began to speak once more of Lucretius, I noticed a fellow student, Marvin Shapiro. Purplish hickeys stood out in the pallor of his face. He was stunned by this reminiscence of death, as I had been, and he too felt that premonitory grief and loneliness. And then he flushed as the blood returned.

After class, I approached and we talked. We cut the rest of our classes that day, strolled the campus, ate ice cream, circled the track, told our stories, listened to our stories, and finally got around to the subject of girls. This led naturally to pitchers of beer at the West End Tavern on Broadway. By closing time we had decided we were lifelong friends, and so we were. Marvin was a skinny boy with bad skin, a deep voice, a surcharged Adam's apple, and a love of beautiful women. I shared the latter ambition, but aimed at poetry and philosophy as the means to the end of perfect love, perhaps many perfect loves. I also told him (me from Lakewood, Ohio) that he was my first Jewish friend. Marvin looked at me as if I must be crazy. He was from Avenue K in Brooklyn. He knew nothing about Lakewood, Ohio.

Expanding our horizons, we organized expeditions to eat eggplant parmigiana on First Avenue and fish sandwiches at Joe's on South Street near the market. We were voyeurs who stopped at every doorway. After peeking, we discussed what it all meant — that's what philosophy was supposed to be. We shambled through the fish market and saw a child idly paddling his hands in a barrel of shrimp, a boy of eight or nine in a corduroy jumper jacket. He had a bored, sallow, pretty Italian face, and he was dipping his hands into the crisp pink shells and letting them spill through his fingers like doubloons in a pirate movie. He was watching the stand for his father. One withered leg was encased in a paraphernalia of shiny metal braces. Marvin's eyes filled with tears. He was shaking his head and tears were rolling down his cheeks. "What's the matter?" I asked him.

"That kid'll never get laid."

Like most young men in those days, we had a handy solution to all our problems with family, college — administrators wanted us to attend classes — and girls, the debris of childhood still cluttering our path. In the war, we were sure to be heroes. Professor Campbell's eyes looking downward, looking inward, had only begun to do the job of education. A few days earlier, cutting classes again, we had seen a dead man propped against a wall near St. Mark's Place. Reality intended to infect us with the imagination of death.

Despite the intoxication of a sudden friendship between adolescent boys, there were still rivalries and family dramas to be played out. After a period of silence ambling past St.-Mark's-in-the-Bouerie, which was not in the Bowery, my friend punched me and sang, "Mama git the hammer, there's a fly on baby's head."

"All she did was she just swatted me, that's my mother," I said. "We're polite in Lakewood, Ohio," and punched him back.

His Adam's apple on the skinny neck seemed to wobble. "Howsoever and nevertheless, as we say in Brooklyn, New York." He stopped. "You deserved a hammer, and so do I, but my *mamaleh* — that's Brooklyn for Mommy — she doesn't swat . . ." He tried to shake off the thought. "Looks hurt. Looks hurt at Dad, too. I hope this war doesn't stop till I get myself some medals."

He recounted in blazing detail his future destruction of Nazi fliers and had the knack of making it seem to Barnard girls like history, not plan. I envied him. He met and conquered girls in subway crowds, on campus walks, wherever he deigned to point his ardent, demanding eyes, his shiny beak, and his disturbed, acne-bothered face. He would take her for a stroll on Riverside Drive and an ice cream at the Columbia

Chemist and not get back to Hartley Hall until after his first morning class. Unless he lurked outside, imagining my envy all though the grimy New York night, I had to assume that he figured out someplace to go with the lady besides the balcony of the Apollo on Forty-second Street.

To even things out, he envied me, too — my lack of "nervousness." He envied me my year of hitchhiking, driving for drunks, working as a busboy on Key Largo, making my getaway from the Ivy League, as he called it, somehow including Brooklyn. No wonder I was calm, he told me; life had not passed me by. All *he* had to his credit was satisfied lust.

Poor Marvin. I was nervous enough. I would have given up the life that had not passed me by for one, two, or three — as many as the genie allowed me — of the girls who strolled with him. I would offer them deep feeling, each and every one. He shrugged. They couldn't resist him, he admitted, but so what? They just liked Marvin and his cheerful rubbing.

It only *seemed* to be mere cheerful rubbing. He needed them, he really needed and wanted girls, this one and that one, each one in particular during her moment. He was born for women. We walked around Van Am Quad in front of our dorm, a little space of brick and grass, endlessly turning in the damp midnight, while he explained, "Some people are ambitious. You wake up and write your poems at dawn —"

"I'll kill myself, I'm so horny —"

"Shut up. I wake up and I know I'll die if I can't squeeze her beautiful body."

"Whose, Marvin?"

"So the next day I take the subway ride at rush hour. I find someone. I sniff her out and wiggle in, sometimes we never even look at each other's face — sometimes we just go to her place . . ."

"What do you talk about?"

He fixed me with a Brooklyn stare, the sort of look to shrink an innocent from Lakewood, Ohio. "Words are just a way of saying things. Button it, kid." He grinned in the darkness. "I tell her how much I need her. I love her. I treasure her. I adore her. I'll do anything for her, more than anything. When I talk like that, lemme tell you, they always listen closely."

"It's not the words?"

"It's the sincerity." The bust of Van Am glistened in the diffused gray of a globe lamp. There were blackout curtains on the dormitory windows nearby, and lights where the V-12 program Navy boys were doing calculus and navigation problems. We talked round and round. Marvin contained a famine that he offered up in tribute to womankind. He didn't hide his need. Skinny, pimply, and ardent, he surrounded women with the gift of his hunger. He gave it freely; they forgave everything. He was an alchemist with a large Adam's apple and a deep voice who knew how to convert desperation into sincerity. Girls could save him and celebrate his future heroism. He climbed the fire escape and crawled through a window if she hesitated. Torn knees and a beaky smile explained all. They ended up grateful to be able to do so much for him. He responded with tenderness and whispers, and then slept like a child. Sometimes he forgot their names. At least that's what he told me.

Then he met Ellen, a Barnard student who wore black woolen dresses, had long black hair, a long maternal figure;

she wept when he took her into the cold bushes, wept when he brought her out, and wept all the way to her parents' apartment when they left it empty for the weekend. Marvin reported, somewhat worried, that she was still weeping when they emerged on a fine, sunny winter afternoon. He had enjoyed the love of a good woman, but he found it wet.

For my own reasons, partly the war, partly the freshman midyear sag, partly my lack of the love of a good, bad, or in-between woman, I told Marvin I wasn't waiting till the end of the school year to go into the Army. He must have spent an unusually damp evening with Ellen, because his response was short and to the point: "Yeah!" The temptress on the jukebox at the West End was giving us an irrelevant command: "Get outta here and get me some money, too . . ."

The war solved the problem of late term papers, of the failures or successes with girls, general impatience with ourselves. We would enlist together and be heroes together. We didn't need to do right, as the jukebox taunt asked, by getting outta there and getting her some money — we could do right by joining the good war.

Before telling his parents, he asked me to spend a night with his family. I expected to be bored — *parents* — but instead, I was amazed. Although a lawyer, Mr. Shapiro was a jaunty man who wore a yachting cap indoors, drank, ate exotic foods, and fished in the nearby waters. He had his own boat. He talked about mizzens and fore and aft; I was learning Latin and French, but had no grasp of yachting. His face was weathered by Long Island Sound. I had never before met a sailing Jew. Mrs. Shapiro was a soft, sweet woman with a small, pretty, girlish face; she read books, listened to Mozart, and smiled at her husband's jokes. He did calisthenics on a bar above the bed in their room. It was a household unlike what I expected in that furniture-filled house on a leafy Brooklyn street. There was also another boy, younger than Marvin, to whom little attention was paid. The first son was the hope of the family. Mr. Shapiro was delighted by the wildness of a son who twisted and dodged in a way that would have hurt him at thirty; at eighteen, he was a charmer. Marvin had fun when I sought Meaning. Even now, when rubbing up against anonymous women in the subway does not seem very stylish, I carry the memory of a lively boy with a swollen Adam's apple, a deep laugh in a skinny body, doted on by his parents, allowing himself any appetite, all pleasures.

Marvin told them we were both in a hurry for the war. This announcement followed a discussion about Orientals in which we all agreed that there was something puzzling about the newspapers' descriptions of how to tell the face of a Japanese — sneaky, yellow, totalitarian — from that of a Chinese. The Chinese face in those days was open, smiling, and democratic. Marvin's father had a wild, high, energetic laugh. He said the objective testimony of witnesses was often unobjective and inaccurate. He liked the way his son was beginning to think.

"Herb and me, we're going in next Monday," Marvin said suddenly. "It's time. Before all the good jobs'll be taken."

His mother dropped a spoon; it made a little chime against her foot. His father socked him on the back and said, "I knew it, why not? You'll rip 'em apart. They'll give up as soon as they get the news." His eyes glittered with envy. Marvin's kid brother looked adoring and pleased. No one fretted about his mother's tears until he kissed her on the neck, and then she sobbed wildly.

The night before we climbed onto the bus to Camp Upton, we bought tickets for *The Skin of Our Teeth*, with Tallulah Bankhead. She wiggled and chanted just for us. If only she knew we were about to go off to die for our country, we both thought, she would have been absolutely indifferent to us anyway. Ellen was not indifferent to Marvin. I knew a girl from Lakewood, now at Wellesley, who felt about me as Tallulah Bankhead did, not as Ellen did about Marvin Shapiro. We shipped out, we were stripped naked, and we began to put on our new lives.

As with girls, so with the war. Marvin seemed to have all the luck. His reflexes and his eyes were sharp. He became what both of us had wanted to be, a fighter pilot. I went to the infantry, and then was assigned to learn Russian. In the periods between drill and study, in advance of providing liaison with our gallant Soviet allies, we deep Russian scholars continued real life by drinking, complaining, and chasing women at the USO. Most of us were successful at the first two projects, less so at the third. I corresponded with Marvin, with Ellen, and with Marvin's mother. He was in England, flying missions over the Continent. I was in wet white Maryland that next winter, doing maneuvers through an American landscape of barns, churches, apple orchards, all traced and spelled in Russian on our maps. O'er the steppes of Maryland I wandered like a wolf, carrying an M-1 rifle, a full pack, and a new vocabulary, prepared to announce to Soviet partisans: "I am an American soldier and your friend — please don't shoot."

Marvin's mother wrote that she missed our coming out to Avenue K in Brooklyn to eat fish on Saturdays. Her husband spent his weekends in his sailboat, digging salt fish out of the salt sea. He was also doing civilian patrol work. She was worried about her son and wanted me to reassure her.

Ellen wrote that she was crazy in love, and he didn't write often enough. So she looked for letters from me, since I was his best friend.

Marvin wrote that English girls were peculiar but cooperative. He was now a first lieutenant, nice silver bars on his jacket. He didn't do it standing up in an alley in Piccadilly. Girls were willing to take him home. They liked PX chocolate, and he was learning to like tea. The girls also liked to rock with him as the bombs fell and the sirens shrieked. "You'd like London," he said, "but it gets noisy."

We were at the age when such matters needed to be shared. Bragging was his right, envy was mine. Marvin was collecting his reward for being a fighter pilot and a man. He dreamed of a girl in a flowing skirt, flowers and sunlight in a field, and also admired the technical skills of the wife of a Pakistani colonel, or perhaps it was an English colonel stationed in India. A detail, not relevant to the basic points of his letters: Get in this war before it's too late!

Poor Marvin's mother, whose innocent boy was practicing the rites of killing and lust.

Poor Ellen, who imagined him pining for her, far away and needing her.

Poor me, crawling around in Russian in the snowbanks and slushy mud of Maryland in winter. Our officers were combat kicked-outs — men so ineffective at actual fighting that they were sent back to train future intelligence officers.

The only one not to be pitied seemed to be Marvin himself, that charmer, his acne drying with spurts of adrenaline, collecting missions and medals and the wives of our allies.

He made captain. The boy quick into the bushes of Riverside Drive was also quick in the sky against the stubby German fighters. Ellen, his mother, and I formed his audience against the backdrop of destruction, explosions and fire, brandy and good jokes. Seen from our distance, the garish light lit his face and made it angelic, made it devilishly smile.

One winter night the 22nd Class returned to Camp Ritchie, the intelligence training post in Maryland, after nearly a week of simulated war in marshes and orchards. We had been frozen and misled; we had been fired upon and tested; we had conducted a strange war among Maryland mountain people to whom we were not allowed to speak English. We needed shaves; we were jittery with stimulants; we smelled bad. Our mission had been a failure because our officer, who had been responsible for a fatal mistake at Anzio, still believed that his own sense of direction was superior to that of a compass. He knew the way; could a compass give him an argument? Consequently we had been lost for three days in a prickly, cutover pine desert. I felt as if ice had been packed into my ears. We had the usual gripes against officers. The nearer enemy became the real enemy. We stood in our long khaki overcoats against a camp stove, smelling the chicken-feather singe of the wool as we tried to get warm, slurping coffee from our mess kits and reading the accumulated mail. Our officer went to sulk because north was not where north used to be in the Alabama National Guard. I tore open my little stack of mail.

A letter from Marvin described a weekend in London. What fun in the blackout. A duke's daughter, he claimed; mentally I made him out a braggart, maybe a liar, but read on, envying. She loved him, she really did. He cared for her a lot, of course, but not that much. Ellen was writing him weepy letters, and he supposed he would have to close now in order to drop her a line.

Ellen wrote to ask if I had heard from Marvin. She was worried. He must be ill or something.

The last letter, the most recent, was from his mother. He had been shot down over Germany; others in the squadron had seen his parachute open, but it was fired on. There seemed to be a hit in the air. Captain Shapiro was presumed dead.

I crawled outside into the snow. I heaved and gagged. I was too old to cry, and not yet old enough; later I might learn again. There was this churning turmoil like seasickness, like jealousy, like lust and dread. A green and brown puddle spread at my feet. The desire to run away, deny, refuse, was eating at the lining of my belly. This pool of sickness was a trivial response to death, I then thought and still believe, but it was all I could manage. The smell sent me lurching away. I remembered Professor Campbell, his head down, contemplating the Fact, and the awe at his silence Marvin and I had shared. I was feeling my own sickness, while Marvin was now feeling nothing. With shame I recalled Dostoyevsky's denunciation of Turgenev: When he watches a shipwreck, children drowning, he notices the hot tears running down his own face. And here I now had only myself. In the midst of this war for which I was merely preparing, I had lost the vividness of life, my friend. I was gagging in the deep, silent Maryland winter, with nearby slush piles, garbage cans, the debris of soldiering and, just beyond, a horizon of scrub and exhausted soil itching through the snow and a white winter sky. The earth was an ache. I saw Marvin's face — grinning, acne-pocked, delighted by life — under his parachute swinging down and then exploded in midair as he hung between heaven and hell. I've seen him there for more than sixty years, and so he will be always.

Like Dostoyevsky's Turgenev, I'm telling a selfish story. After grief, after washing the stink out of my mouth, how does the vain young poet survive? He writes a vain young poem, of course. It was a long elegy to the memory of Captain Marvin Shapiro (1924–1945) typed in the company orderly room at Camp Ritchie, Maryland, and mailed to *The Atlantic Monthly*, 8 Arlington Street, Boston, Massachusetts. Presently it was returned with a letter signed by a woman who praised . . . something; who was kind to the soldier. I haven't seen the poem since the war. I remember its shape on the page, not the words. Surely the editor wrote to me only because I was a soldier mourning a dead friend and there was a war on. Shortly afterward, I shipped out and lost the poem. I carried the letter from Marvin's mother with me.

His body was never recovered. He had written to me that it was odd to have the *H* initial on his dog tags, Hebrew, when he might need to parachute into Germany; but he kept the initial. Anyway, he was destroyed in the sky.

The Columbia College class of '46 returned to begin again as twenty-one-year-old sophomores. We counted our losses and secretly watched out of the corners of our eyes those with missing limbs or pink, still-healing scars. Some were in line for plastic surgery; some were outpatients; many were on partial disability pensions. Our hairlines had changed. Moony faces were lean and loony. There was confusion, the G.I. Bill, and a host of baby eighteen-year-olds who claimed to be college students, too. No more dormitory living for me. I rented a room on West 113th Street off Broadway and thought to enter adult life after the years of murderous limbo. Our bodies twitched with unfulfilled destruction. How dare we live, how dare we not live. On behalf of world peace and understanding, a friend and I jumped a thuggish heckler at a street-corner Henry Wallace rally. We formed a kleptobibliomaniacal society, stealing books, cheese, things small and large that we could use or give away. We called it the Book Find Club. Our motto was: Steal four books and get a fruitcake free from the A&P. We initiated our girlfriends into the club. In their own confusion they thought the war heroes must know what they were doing. They thought we were heroes and nervous. We were more nervous than heroic.

The mere babies who were our classmates could dress in their Ivy League tweed jackets from J. Crew, their rep ties from wherever rep ties were striped; proudly we flaunted our khakis, our field jackets, and our paratroop boots if we'd been able to liberate them. Some veterans earnestly took up the pursuit of sensible jobs and family life, skipping late adolescence in favor of midcentury adulthood, oncoming gray flannel suits. Another cohort, bruised or merely defiant, ran wild through Manhattan, keeping the chip on our shoulders carefully balanced. This wildness, after all, was that of college boys on the G.I. Bill.

Besides world peace and understanding, I practiced the stealing of books from chain bookstores, war profiteer bookstores, evil *capitalist* bookstores, and then stealing them onto the dusty shelves of a bookseller whose kind face I liked — I deigned to approve of him. Among the weak and distressed, the confused and resentful — and there I was, along with other pre-beatnik beatniks — playing God was an act we enjoyed. It was our right and duty. I've lost track of my vinyl 78 rpm record, "Hitler Lives!" of a country western song by a genius I remember as Red River Dave. In an angry twang he snarled, "Hitler lives if you turn a vit-run from your door . . . Hitler lives!"

To be a tragic sophomore at age twenty-one did not give me the moral right to adopt Red River Dave's anthem as mine. It was not an instance of Nazi oppression to be grabbed by the shoulder by a security guard on the crowded sidewalk outside the Scribner's bookshop on Fifth Avenue. Under my U.S. Army field jacket I was hiding a copy of *The Place of Value in a World of Fact* by a profound German thinker who may have been Austrian or Swiss. The Puerto Rican security guard, emphasizing my guilt, magnifying my punishment, didn't let me buy the book. But despite vengeful security guards and adverse registration in the now-defunct Scribner's bookshop records, I sincerely wanted to find the place of value in the factual world.

When an innocent non-veteran asked Moochie, one of the Book Find Club crew, if Moochie was a girl's name, it would have been enough to say, "No, it's mine." But instead he kicked the questioner in the crotch and inquired, "A girl ever do that to you?" I suggested he call himself Moocher instead — a more manly suffix.

Along with my thoughts of Marvin, on whose behalf I was taking revenges against the world, whose habits I was sometimes imitating, I came gradually to think of his mother, his father, and Ellen. Busy installing myself in bohemian student days, sullen, selfish, and arrogant, I didn't know how to deal with the grief of others. But finally, as the months went by, I decided to visit Marvin's family. I telephoned Mrs. Shapiro and she reminded me of how to get to Avenue K by subway. I used to know the way. My ears felt different in the roar of the tunnel.

At the subway entrance I began to think of the smoked eel I had eaten for the first time at their house. He had said, bragging, "We have eels all the time — crabs, lobsters, oysters, shrimp. Snails. Clams."

"Do you eat pork?" I asked.

"*Feh*, unclean," he had said.

I remembered pausing at the newsstand to pick up a copy of *PM*. It was the same guy with the stacks of papers, fret on his face, hair in his ears, waiting out his time.

I expected the house to be dark with mourning. Instead, it was light and sunny, curtains pulled back and winter sunlight filling the rooms. But it seemed empty. Even some of the furniture was gone. It was emptied of its men. After his death, Marvin's father had enlisted, not as a lawyer, but as an expert sailor, and had commanded a landing craft and had fought as an overage captain through southern France. At the end of the war, he simply didn't return. Mrs. Shapiro, smiling, told me that he met a girl in Marseilles. I couldn't imagine what a Brooklyn lawyer would do in Marseilles — Jean Gabin yes, Mr. Shapiro no — and I saw him in a corduroy cap, on the waterfront, a handsome, stocky, middle-aged settler with a young, high-breasted Fifi with wooden soles on her shoes and a black market Pall Mall hanging from her lips.

Mrs. Shapiro said simply, "It broke up our family. We were a good family, I think, but we needed Marvin." Her other son was now at Yale, very white-shoe, probably in a J. Crew or Brooks jacket, rep tie.

She made tea. We talked about Marvin. Tea, raisin toast, orange marmalade, chocolate cookies. I thought of Marvin's hickeys —"zits," the freshmen now called them. She told me a little about her marriage and, I knew, would later want to tell me more. My need for a community of mourning gave way to embarrassment. I could not be husband and son to her, and when I slipped out into the deep early night, I tried to feel sadness and sympathy. I felt sympathy and sadness, and relief to escape. Marvin was my friend in the past. What community I sought could not be built from nostalgia.

Still, I wanted to find Ellen. When I finally met her again, she was also in mourning, wearing an ugly, shapeless woolen dress and flat shoes, her hair untended, smelling of pain and poor caring. She was a graduate student with a reputation for persistent moping. Never a pretty girl, she had been a sweetly attractive one. Now at age twenty-three, she looked ravaged, left out in bad weather. I had a bit more patience with her than with Marvin's mother. We took coffee and meals together near campus. She wanted to drink at the West End because she had gone there so often with Marvin and me. Three times, I think. She imagined for herself the history of a great love; she imported it backward into time; she imagined widowhood. At first I shared the play, stunned by her conception of him, which seemed so much deeper than my own. They had been truly in love, they had been profound true lovers; it was not just wrestling in the grass of

Riverside Drive, it was not couch work in her parents' apartment on Central Park West, it was an immortal passion. Her hero had been blasted out of the skies by malevolent fate and she would treasure his memory forever. Marvin and Ellen stood in the great tradition of doomed lovers. She was a graduate student in literature.

After a few immersions in her dream of the past, I began to feel discomfort and then resentment. Marvin had been my best friend, and memory of him made me ache. But the person I knew slipped away in the tumult of Ellen's ardent dream. I found new resources of coldness in myself. I would watch impatiently for her to finish her beer and then deliver her to her room on Amsterdam Avenue. Once when she managed to order another beer, I felt ready to groan with boredom. And when she wanted me to come to her room, tiptoeing past the other rooms, past the common kitchen, I felt as if I were being led into a trap. Suddenly there were wet, beery kisses. I twisted away and cried out, "You're lying to yourself! Never cared about you! He had girls everywhere, England, Brooklyn, everywhere!"

She started to run down the darkened hall. I caught her at the door, held her in my arms as she struggled, and pointed out that it was not my room that she was running from, but her own. She should stay and I should go. Make sense, please. I'm sorry, but it's the truth.

I believed myself to be rational, logical, surgical, but also I was breathing the stench of a woman's hysteria for the first time in my life. Little popping explosions of rage and hatred were going off in my arms. "You think you can play God! You think you're God and my judge!" she shrieked at me.

The practice of playing God and judge sometimes exhausts itself with time. I have the disease worse than most (*Ellen, wherever you are*).

I dragged her back to her room. Invisible ears were pressed to the shut bedroom doors. Community kitchen, community crises. Shush, shush, I said. The stringent, leaping sobs subsided; she was simply weeping; I put her in bed with her clothes on, covered her, and sat stroking her hand. Toward dawn she fell asleep. Cold-eyed I felt. I tiptoed out.

Back on the street, I saw a metal case of milk at the door of a short-order restaurant. For the first time in my life — not the last — I had spent a night trying to calm a woman made mad by something I had said. And for the last time in my life I felt that, well, it wasn't my fault at all, I was right, I had done the right thing, I was right. So I told myself. So I told myself again. Still insisting, I believed that I had committed an obscenity. I stood at the doorway of the diner: CLOSED. GO AWAY.

They had no right to be rude. I was hungry and thirsty. I was a veteran. They were turning a veteran from their door.

The metal case of milk glittered in the early light. I bent to the bottles. My hand felt a sensual coolness, like touching a loved woman. It would be sweet to drink long, cool swallows and then heave the bottle into the street. I was thirsty and hungry and cold and feverish, and I decided not to steal a bottle of milk.

I stood there, squinting at the metal case. I would leave it in a moment. I would leave without a bottle for myself. This was a new decision. The night had brought me much that was new.

When next I saw Ellen, she had changed her hair, cut it stylishly, and her clothes seemed to be freshly dry-cleaned. She was a handsome twenty-three-year-old woman. She was going with someone. She had a *friend*. We met as acquaintances, students who used to know each other. She made it clear that I had sacrificed our friendship. She smiled and inquired about my doings. I had little to say to her. Our life together was all in the past. I had projects for the future. She was married within the year, gave up graduate work, got pregnant, left New York. Though I insisted to myself that I had done the right thing, she made me uncomfortable. It was much easier not to see her on campus.

Now the years have passed, and I think of my friend who died when he and I were mere children. The event still seems real when I remember it, but like a reality glimpsed through thick glass.

Sometimes, however, when an immediate grief breaks the glass of memory, Marvin comes tumbling free and alive again under his parachute. The distancing of history is reversed. I am accustomed to his death. And yet, when I needed an occasion to express grief at something else, at something happening to me, in my own life, I found Marvin waiting like a boy, ready to play. I told his story to a friend who was an infant when he flew over Germany. "He was dead before he had time to lose his acne." I had no tears for Marvin's mother or Ellen, but now, telling it, I struggled for control of myself.

My friend reminded me coolly, "Ellen's a grandmother by now. Marvin's father, do you think he's still in Marseilles? No more eels for that one. His mother must be gone, too. His kid brother . . ."

"A retired prof, I heard."

"So," she said. "So it was a long time ago."

Yes, child, that was mere history. There are always new wars for which we must prepare ourselves, and I am still ready. I'm also ready to join the company of O. J. Campbell, remembering my own deaths.

5

The Norwegian Captain

One of the ephemeral predators who ruled Haiti, a colonel self-promoted to general, also a self-credentialed philosopher in his tailored white uniform with glorious philosopher epaulets, medals, and braid, commented from the height of the mountain of murders over which he presided: "Haiti is a land where life is more terrible than death." The distinctions others felt about life and death left Colonel-General-Philosopher-Coup-Leader Cedras with a stoic indifference, although he seemed to enjoy his own scuba diving and dominion over eight million souls.

Foreigners, it seemed, had the luxury of taking life and death seriously. The man at the ironwork balcony might have looked like a handsome sea-stained old Viking — white fringe of beard, stalwart hairy nose and ears — but the Norwegian captain was a mere annoyance as far as my buddy Whitley, the art dealer, was concerned. Just stationing himself at the Pension Croft in Jacmel, just taking his morning coffee and bread in the lobby, spending the day looking down toward the market or out toward the Caribbean Sea from the balcony of his room, just doing nothing at all, day after day after day — not even seizing the chance to pick up some

Haitian art at a good price from Whitley — the Norwegian captain was a total violation of the proper order of things. The old bore displayed too much cartilage and too much gloom.

Why come to Haiti, Whitley asked, unless you buy a Haitian primitive painting or two? Why lurk about this dysparadise with no fun in your heart, no spending of money on genuine folk art that could almost be guaranteed to increase in value?

He tried to remedy the situation. The Norwegian captain resisted the remedy. For Whitley, there developed a distressing condition of pissed-off impasse as he showed various canvases and promised they could be packed and wrapped for easy handling on the captain's eventual flight back to Oslo. "Look, flowers and mountains . . . look, stand back a step, the characteristic flat perspective, the spirit of this island, but also a certain ebullience —"

"Ebullience?" asked the captain.

"Joie de vivre," said Whitley, wondering if this was a concept that existed in Norway.

"Thank you so much, but why?" the captain asked. He stood with the cautious dignity of a man guarding against old-age confusion, that combination of deafness, slowed reflexes, the world distorted by sore back and worried brain. "What would I do with such a painting?"

"Show it to your friends."

"Who?"

"Put it on your wall."

"Where?"

Whitley was losing patience. "You must live someplace. You must have friends. What about cousins? Or maybe a . . ."

And he used an odd word for a son or daughter: "A descendant? You've got some of those?"

"Who?" asked the captain. "Where?"

I guessed that he was a man who spent much of his time on the sea, and was home long enough to have children but perhaps did not, and expected an old age with a wife who would wait patiently for history to fulfill itself, giving them each other forever. And when it didn't work out that way, he traveled to Haiti, along with others whom history had deceived. And when even Port-au-Prince wasn't far enough from home, he found his way around the island to the village of Jacmel, where ships used to load coffee and sisal, but now the harbor had filled with silt and ships stopped only to let the naked stevedores wade out to offload rice or canned milk and sometimes a narcotics trafficker or a lost soul in search of a redeeming Strange. To be alone in faraway ports was an old habit for the Norwegian captain.

He stood watching us from the narrow ironwork balcony of the Pension Croft as we hoisted a bag with sandwiches and water into the jeep.

History had brought Whitley to the island for different reasons. It was the place where he could work out his dreams and evade the expectations of his parents and nanny. A kid from Princeton (family trusts well past their peak, capital eroded), a marginal littérateur but a first-rate tennis player, he very wisely settled on a niche life in tropical Haiti. There was year-round good tennis and no stooping or chasing for balls. There were dollar-a-day ball boys. The available sex before the time of AIDS was an additional plus. He developed an expertise in the emerging culture of primitive art. He got in on the ground floor. With his good Princeton manners, plus the kind of ear filter that prevented registering complaints about his behavior, he got away with buying Haitian art cheaply, touting the artists he had picked, writing little articles in alumni and art magazines, then unloading his inventory to collectors. He wanly emulated in the art trade the techniques of the stock-promoting forebears to whom he was indebted for his trust fund.

When he couldn't sell a painting, he could sometimes give it to a museum — especially local and college museums stimulated by his authoritative articles on folk art — at tax valuations set by the art-dealing equivalent of his tennis service in the back court. He was an expert.

During a period of spousal support stress, a tragic fire consumed most of his personal collection. Some of the lost paintings were lively, funny, touching, lovely, no matter how exaggerated their valuations for insurance purposes. My unkind suspicions about the fire convinced me that he didn't even much care for the art about which he was an expert. It was just something to do.

Perhaps I have already revealed that I wasn't fond of him. When we played tennis, he could never manage to serve from behind the baseline.

Once I asked Whitley about accepting the loan of a jeep and a driver from Papa Doc, President-for-Life Dr. François Duvalier, and then writing a magazine article about the brutal dictatorship in which he declared that Dr. Duvalier was at last giving voice to the poor of Haiti who had always been oppressed by the mulatto elite.

"Is that a critical, Herb?"

"Oh, no, nothing like that."

He paused to gather his thoughts. "It's time for the black shits to get something from the brown shits."

I never summoned up enough rudeness to question his multifaceted art dealing: buying, promoting, selling, donating, insuring, and burning. If I did, he would call all my tennis drives out instead of only the ones close to the baseline. "Like to place a little bet, make things a little more interesting in this heat?" he gently inquired in the soft monotone he used for understated, well-bred persuasion.

We bet five gourdes, which at that time in the late sixties was fixed at a dollar. For me, it was worth five gourdes to see how the bet affected his serve. With a dollar at stake, he served with *both* feet over the baseline. He probably could have beaten me anyway, but for Whitley, winning wasn't enough; playing the game according to the rules of others was a violation of his personal code. He needed to show me, the world, and the ghosts of his history who was boss. He also liked taking the five gourdes; a person can always find something to do with them. This baby was a winner.

Only in Haiti would Whitley and I have been tennis partners, even something like buddies. We were two *blancs* on an isolated island, sharing an interest in tennis, primitive art, and the tragicomedy of Haitian history. Under the circumstances it seemed like a lot to have in common, even though we had little in common.

Today my friend Whitley was more than usually exasperated. He had given the benefit of his expert counsel to the stupid captain and the stupid captain had still said no. He just stood there. He looked at Whitley, impenetrable. He seemed not to understand anything Whitley explained about investment in artistic genius and future resale value. Whitley hated it when a person persisted in his own irrelevant distractions while Whitley was giving him the lowdown on indigenous culture.

"Perhaps after I think about this," said the captain.

"Personally, I don't think you will," said Whitley.

Some people have no esthetic judgment, nor do they want any help. Not young anymore, Whitley retained the urgent, rosy, youthful glow of a person who needs to get his own way and occasionally doesn't, but at least he could feel good about not abasing himself. He didn't have to pretend anymore. He could abandon himself to his natural pleasure in disliking someone who didn't come up to his standards.

He seemed to have reservations about me, too, and I couldn't blame him. He asked: "Maybe I'm wasting my time being your friend?"

I didn't answer.

"You're saying you're not my friend, Herb?"

"I didn't say anything."

He gazed at me with mild, almost amorous satisfaction. "At last the lad speaks. That's what you're telling me, am I right?" He grinned and stared, his lips slightly parted as if he were out of breath. "And I can hear your footsteps trotting away, very clearly, trot-trot, trot-trot, although you think you're still standing right here. Isn't that what a true artist does? Or a true critic of art who devotes his life to it? Hear or paint what hasn't happened yet?"

Maybe the spirit of decency was prowling around Whitley, making it difficult for him to be what he was; or if not decency, at least tenderness, a vibration of hurt and need that expressed itself as hurt, need, and anger. Once meeting him for tennis, I came to his gallery and found him touching a sculpture by André Dimanche — a crucifix with Agoué, the god of water, soldered across it — caressing Agoué lightly with his fingers. He muttered, "Caught," with an embarrassed little laugh, as if he knew what I was thinking: He must really care for it! He does!

"This one I might not sell," he said. "It belongs in my permanent collection, *semi*-permanent, because I might not live forever, pal."

"I'm sure you will."

"Ha-ha. How about the one who loses a bet on that pays for the rum punches at the funeral of the other? And maybe the horse doovers, too."

Hors d'oeuvres. He was still embarrassed, hiding behind his Princeton boy kidding. He didn't like to be considered softhearted, although there wasn't much danger of it. Instead, I was wondering if he regretted the temptations of an insurance fire. He may have had a sneaking affection for me, as he did for the sculptor André Dimanche. He'd mind if I went out in flames; there was no reason to insure my survival. But as to the Norwegian captain — that boy could just go fuck himself and his walls in Oslo, which were probably decorated with sailing prints, maps, and a compass.

It happened that Whitley and I were visiting the village of Jacmel, across the peninsula to the south of Port-au-Prince, at the same time. Jacmel was once a major coffee exporting port, and with land communication as poor as it was, people used to say it was easier to get from Jacmel to Paris by ship than from Jacmel to Port-au-Prince by road. Known for its grace and elegance, its isolation, a provincial sweetness, Jacmel occasionally — not often — enjoyed the convenience of electricity. A few jeeps or all-terrain vehicles bounced through the streets scattering donkeys, children, and Mesdames Saras, market women, their burdens on their heads. For more than fifty years, Préfète Duffaut was painting his dream images of the town — mountain, sea, winding paths, wooden gingerbread houses with vines curling toward jeweled towers. The coffee trade has vanished, but art miners still come to visit and carry away ironwork crosses, fish, and images of Damballah, the great snake god, or lamps, chandeliers, and toys made of milk cans, or paintings by Préfète Duffaut and all the little Duffautlings who imitate the master (Duffaut was imitating himself these days, too).

It didn't matter what Whitley thought of me and I thought of him. We were two white Americans in this faraway village, and therefore we looked to each other something like colleagues. I had rented a jeep for a climb into the countryside to visit the shrine of Ci-va-Dieu, the pool and waterfall that was a voodoo Lourdes, a holy place of prayer, healing, and reconciliation. Whitley asked to go with me; how could I not take him? We were sitting in the open vehicle outside the Pension Croft when the warmhearted proprietor, everybody's auntie, came running out into the sun, something she normally avoided, not wanting to darken her coffee-colored skin. One of her ancestors was a Frenchwoman, Caroline Levy, whose straight hair grew almost to her ankles. Madame had proved this to me with a faded photograph, but then said it was easy for her grandmother to grow her hair so long —"elle était petite petite petite, et si mignonne, regardez, Monsieur."

Now an important matter had brought her out into the morning sun. "That European, the *blanc* in the front room," she said.

"I already know him," Whitley said.

The *blanc* was standing at the little iron balcony, staring out toward the sea — a thin old man, once tall, now less tall, with his fringe of yellowish beard and a visored woolen cap of a sort, which made no sense in this climate, the dark wool drawing heat into the head. He looked over and past us, not asking any notice from his two fellow *blancs* in the jeep. Madame said: "He is waiting for nothing. He has been here a month now, that's all he does. He waits and stands there — *ça m'agace*. Please, you have room in your jeep, take him with you." And she leaned forward to whisper: "His wife died. He came to Haiti to try to forget."

People did this, folks used Haiti in this way, alcoholics, addicts, victims, criminals on the lam, people who were suffering and wanted to escape to a place that made no connection with anything they had known before. After his wife died, the Norwegian captain came to stand on a balcony in Jacmel.

Whitley looked at me, incredulous, as I jumped out of the jeep. I called up toward the balcony, "Sir? May I come upstairs?"

The door was ajar, but he seemed to have forgotten I was on my way. He was still standing at the cast iron railing with its eroded and salt-rusted fretwork. He was gazing past the harbor toward the open sea, beyond where I had stood when I called to him. Perhaps the door was open only to draw the breeze, not to invite me in. "Sir?" I said.

There were photographs in frames stationed about the room and an unframed photograph lying on the bed. His wife had been a plump, round-cheeked, elderly woman, not a Viking princess. I stepped into the room and found myself looking at the photograph next to the pillow with the solicitous indifference of someone pretending to admire baby pictures. "Sir," I said, "you might like to visit this place. They think it's magic. There are ceremonies, they bathe and invoke the gods."

Slowly he turned the bony face with its straggle of beard toward me. He was aware, but it was as if he were moving under water, not swimming but turning in the tug of tide.

"It's called Ci-va-Dieu," I said.

"Here comes God," he answered.

"You speak Creole?"

"Some words are very like French. Dieu va ici. Ci-va-Dieu. But it means there goes God or here comes God?"

He followed me down the narrow stairway that led into the ground floor reception area where breakfast would be served if one took breakfast, where street musicians played in the evening if Madame invited them in to play. Whitley sat in the jeep, expressing impatience by not taking comfort in the shade while he waited for me. He was wearing a floppy tropical travel hat to protect his heavily freckled face.

The Norwegian captain said, "Thank you very much, sir. Yes, thank you."

When he climbed into the back, Whitley seemed to decide he only spoke Norwegian. Whitley asked, "Who's paying for this jeep?"

"I am, don't worry, you're not," I said. I had rented it for the day.

"Well, he should pay his share anyway."

I was thinking of the prices I had paid for things, thinking of my own loss, which had brought me to Haiti this time, a divorce, a debit that was drastic for me but so much less than the Norwegian captain's loss.

"He's out there just when we're going someplace interesting. What a co*inky*dink."

"*Coinkydink.* Was that a Nassau Street word in your time?"

"My second wife liked to say that. No girls at Princeton when I was there — how the devil can anybody learn anything these days? We were only crazed on weekends, I suppose now they're crazed all the time. Figures, doesn't it?"

I felt startled and sunstruck by this irritable rambling about suspicious coincidence, origin and pronunciation of a word or cute babytalk for a word, the passing of the tradition of all-male colleges, the many marriages of my buddy Whitley. He had been at Princeton when only gentlemen could be found there. Now here he was having to deal with an island of non-gentlemen and an imperfectly civilized individual from his own country. He pulled at the soft brim of his sun hat, tugging it down around his forehead and ears. I decided not to point out that it resembled an oversized yarmulke, and having made my decision, then heard myself cheerfully remarking to him: "Israelis wear a hat looks just like that."

The moment of falling in love sometimes strikes like an accident of tropical storm — her hand brushes mine in passing and then falls away and then swiftly returns. Similarly, the moment when spite changed to something like pity for Whitley came when he complained, insisting, "Then he must pay for his share of the jeep!" Though the cost was mine, Whitley felt personally aggrieved. He had given up on the captain. He wanted me to himself during this outing when he hoped to overcome my unhidden dislike of him and perhaps his of me. Maybe he only wanted an ally in the business of art promotion, not a friend, but nevertheless he seemed pinched and bereft. He, too, was sensitive to loss.

Between Whitley and me there was the bond of travelers, on edge, wide-awake, a little lonely. Dr. Duvalier, the crazed Président-à-Vie, had lent him a jeep and now I did, too, but my loan wasn't free and clear. He had to share it with that dreary Norwegian who had made really bad choices in life, wearing a stupid black woolen cap, refusing to invest in terrific works of art, and loving a wife who died. "Hey, change your mind maybe?" Whitley called over his shoulder, but the captain didn't seem to hear him.

The noise of rattling vehicle and rushing wind drowned our conversation as we bounced on a dried-mud road, grinding in low gear up a steep slope past little clusters of *caille-pailles*, the peasant mud and straw huts. Naked children, bellies forward, chased us, screaming with laughter. Droning of wind, high-pitched laughter, shrieks of it; and the Norwegian captain silent on the metal seat in the back of the jeep. Madame from the Pension Croft had given us a bag of crab sandwiches and bottles of water; I worried about what crabmeat and mayonnaise would find to do in this heat.

★   ★   ★

Often in Haiti, history and accidents just seem to occur, growing out of volcanic hillsides like the rocks that suddenly come to birth one morning, glinting in the sunlight after the slow churning of night. It's not magic; it just happens again and again. A cooperative work rite, the *coumbite*, labors to clear the land with a crew of diggers and haulers, an admiral to blow a whistle or pipe the bamboo tube, a general to beat the drum. Work is better done with music; the musicians solemnly perform their part of the task. The last time I visited Ci-va-Dieu, years ago, there had been a *coumbite* on the slope nearby; there was one now, too, gathering the rocks for a fence and making room on a hillside for corn to grow. "They sing," said the Norwegian captain. Whitley scowled under his floppy hat, his mood compounded of heat, sweat, and annoyance with our guest's banality.

Suddenly the air changed, freshened. I pulled the jeep to the side of the path, and we continued on by foot toward the waterfall with its sweet shedding of coolness from high in the hills at Cap Rouge, or from coursing down the stream of La Gosseline, or from the Étang — I'm not sure of the geology here. Folks were bathing, there was the chime of song, the pleasant chirping and laughing of children, their smiles intensified by freshness, the blessing of water, especially this sanctified water. A lovely young girl, droplets pearling on her skin, gleaming, stood in a pool, holding her newborn child and crooning to him. I thought it was some sort of blessing, but then heard the words: "Fais dodo, Kola mon petit frère, fais dodo, tu auras du gâteau." *Sleep my child, little brother Kola, go to sleep, and later you'll eat cake.* Not a blessing but a children's song; a blessing anyway.

"She's not singing in Creole," Whitley said. It was a

complaint, as if he were somehow foiled. "It's pidgin French. It's old French. Where'd she learn those words?"

"In another life," I suggested, "or maybe from her mother or her mother's mother."

"Or the radio," Whitley said. "Transistors all over the map."

The Norwegian captain turned his face from Whitley to me and then back to the girl singing naked in the pool. After a while we headed back single file on a narrow path of rocks and trampled mud. A little crowd had gathered around the jeep, poking it with their hands as if they were testing an animal. *"Bonjour blancs! bonjour blancs!"* They stared and smiled and scrambled off the path as I navigated the slope to get the jeep facing the way out. They shouted advice, urging me backward and forward, and then stood laughing and waving and enjoying our departure as they had enjoyed our visit.

"I like this merry place," the captain suddenly said in his English that seemed to be learned from an old children's book. "As a ghost, it's so bright, I am happy to haunt this place."

Whitley looked amazed. "Hey, that's the picture," he said. "I could ask one of my artists to paint that scene. You could be Agoué. Your *hat*. Would you like to commission such a painting?"

The captain looked up. He wasn't sure he understood.

"The god of the sea," I said. "Agoué is Neptune, maybe, or Moses, or Saint Christopher — something like that."

"Those are not the same thing at all," said the captain severely. He squinted at me in the sunlight, seeing a man whose gods were in a jumble. Then he took to staring at a little compound of *caille-pailles*, cooking fires burning with the smells of cane and charcoal, voices gathered in the shade of palm trees. The children howled with joy at the jeep thrusting and jumping with its disheveled passengers, dusty and foolish, one wearing a floppy Abercrombie yarmulke. *"Bonjour blancs! Bonjour blancs!"*

As we bounced down the road, really just a rutted dried-mud path, Whitley took pleasure in chatting with me in a way that firmly excluded the Norwegian captain. Our passenger sat gazing out at the palms, the scrub and vines, the *caille-pailles*, and the people who stood by, calling out *"Blanc, blanc."* "The important thing used to be finding emotion in painting. Modern art leaves that out. It doesn't even tell the story anymore, so consumers buy whatever they think . . ." A child stepped in front of us and I had to brake suddenly as the naked girl with her distended belly put her hand out, saying, "Fi-cens, *blanc*, gee mee fi-cens." Whitley went on as soon as we were back in gear: "Poor people hang cheap kitsch, rich people buy expensive kitsch or pretend they *really* want high art at the level they can afford. They hire experts. They don't know what they like, but they know what's good." He snorted with his joke. "*Outsider* art — so what's the opposite? Insider art? But I'll tell you, dear colleague, there's something honest in naïve — folk — primitive — what the fuck, it's *real*, so what shall we call it?"

The captain was staring into the scrub as if he wanted it made clear that he wasn't eavesdropping on us. Reddish dust glistened in his reddish white beard.

"— and I'm lucky enough to do pretty well professionally, besides. How many can say that?" Whitley smiled thinly, the dust smearing his lips, changing to a smear of mud as he licked and spat into a cloth. "As well as I can." More smile; wiping of mouth. "Better all the time."

"Do you care for Haitian painting?" I called into the wind, turning my head toward the captain.

"I believe so," he said, and I didn't ask what question he thought he was answering. Then we were all three, even Whitley, distracted by a large black junk bird hopping from low bush to low bush with a part of its wing and a piece of a leg chewed off by some predator. No one said anything until the jeep was safely past and the captain said, "A cat, I think."

"More likely a rat," said Whitley.

There was a gloom in Whitley that made me want to unlock him, an utterly forlorn meanness, which rapidly alternated with his bursts of salesmanship, his waves of manic enthusiasm for the pitch. The captain's darkness was filled with ghosts. It was grief unrelenting. It wanted to take total possession of him; it spilled into the corners of his mouth and the reddened eyelids; but he sat there vigilant, a hero against himself. I watched him study his hand as he lifted and held it in the air, pretending to shield himself against the sun, looking for the tremor of loss of control. In the gesture I could imagine his patient lovemaking over the years with the sweet round-cheeked lady in the photographs in his room at the Pension Croft.

It was impossible to imagine Whitley losing himself, crying out in a moment of joining soul and body with another's. The captain, at the edge of very old age, was both a passionate man and burnt out, those qualities joined in him. Whitley, greedy, tirelessly needy, was a person I thought I knew and still a mystery to me.

Back at the Croft, the captain's scalp under the coppery white hair gleamed with sunburn, his skin weathered and reddened afresh. He climbed down from the jeep and stood alongside, trying to figure out why Whitley was angry. He gave up. He said to us both, "The best day, the very best. Thank you very much."

Then he entered the hotel and Whitley said, "At least you should have asked him for his share of the gas."

"I told you," I said.

"And I told *you*."

"Okay, okay, I need a nap. Too much sun."

"I didn't have my nap this afternoon and I'm older than you are."

"Are you collecting errors these days, along with art?" I asked, and finally he shut up. He was handing out reproaches free of charge, a steady barrage of them, but in this heat, at the end of a long day, no one could expect perfect affability.

The next morning, very early, on my way to the market, I watched a procession of children, girls in matching red and blue jumper dresses, heading to school for some sort of ceremony. The red and blue were patriotic colors, standing for the unity of Haiti. (According to legend, the Haitian flag had been created by tearing the white out of a red, white, and blue banner; the national logic defined the mulatto as red and the black as blue.) It was barely dawn; streaks of pink and white in the sky. Things start early so that things can close down at noon when the blasting midday furnace takes over. Again I heard that chattering and laughter that make some North Americans and Europeans envy the Haitian talent for pleasure despite the long disaster of Haitian history. Pleasure seemed especially stubborn in Jacmel.

I was looking for presents for my children at the beach-side market — a dress sewn from many-colored scraps for my daughter, with lace around the collar and decorative buttons in improbable places, in crooked rows down the sleeves; a wooden bird carved from driftwood for a son; a painting of chickens eating corn for another son. I thought of buying something for my wife, my soon-to-be-ex-wife, but I wasn't sure she would think it appropriate. I was thinking of other early mornings with her, when everything we did together was appropriate.

Then I went back for breakfast at the Croft, a glass of *shadek*, grapefruit juice, and the strong dark-roasted Haitian coffee with canned condensed milk, and the coarse white bread with its fresh, raw, sour taste, which I loved. I flung my packages down and sat at the little bar in the hall.

The bread was on a platter on the counter, cut in thick chunks, but before I could reach for it, Madame la Patronne asked, "What shall we do?"

I followed her upstairs. The Norwegian captain's door was ajar. A man in a red neckerchief, red shoes, maybe dressed for his daughter's school celebration, was standing fastidiously a few steps from the bed. His red bandanna was also the emblem of voodoo priests and *tontons macoutes*. The official was the District Something, sheriff, *chef de section*, probably also the coroner. The captain's mouth was open against the pillow and the pillow was wet around it.

"Translate, please," said the man with the red bandanna. I wondered why the captain wrote to his wife in English, not Norwegian, on the scrap of paper: *I loved you, I loved you.* And that was all he wrote. It may not have been a farewell letter; it may only have been a conversation interrupted by death.

The photographs of his wife were wrapped in copies of *Le Nouvelliste*, the oldest newspaper in Haiti, which still looked as if it were printed on handset type. I doubt that the captain had been sick. He had tied the package of photographs with rough hemp twine from the marketplace down the street. There was an Oslo address on the package and a small bundle of currency, dollars and gourdes, slipped under the knotted cord. By the time I turned back after looking around the room to see that he had packed his clothes, the money was gone. The official was writing something on the back of a child's school tablet. He met my eyes with bland, peaceful, bureaucratic complacency, daring me to ask where the money went. In Jacmel, among strangers, in the time of Papa Doc, I was not going to ask this question.

"If you permit, Monsieur," I said, "I could mail these photographs to Norway from Miami when I leave."

"Monsieur le *Notaire*," he said, correcting me about the matter of his office and proper title. It wasn't a direct answer. I felt a little nervous about proposing to carry away the package without his express permission.

There was a heavy smell of bodies in that room, some living, some not; dust, sweat, and the accumulating heat of the morning. Whitley had come up silently behind me, hearing the disturbance one floor down from his room. He was rakishly barefooted, Princeton boy investigating events down the hall in his dorm.

"Personally, my private opinion," he said, "all we did was upset his routines — accomplished nothing. Tried to do something for a person and you see? You see what happens?"

"What happens?"

Whitley bent fastidiously toward the bed — not afraid to get too close — and then peeked up at me, hoping to move my education along. "I showed him a zombie, it was really beautiful work — Gourgue, one of my best painters, moonlight in the cemetery, the peasant leading the zombie by a rope — not expensive for a fabulous piece. Problem was, he was a zombie himself."

"What happens?"

In a close and crowded room, the captain lying there in his silence, Whitley saw that he had my attention. "What happens was that we wasted our time. We should have known. A person doesn't love life, he isn't going to love this fantastic folk art."

6

Adolescence Can Strike at Any Age

Senile sex, let's take that bull by the priapic horn. Sentimentality about old lovers increases with age, time returning the widowed and wizened to days of carefree lust, even if it wasn't all that carefree. A time-honored aphrodisiac from before the Viagra conquest was said to be the touch of a lover's hand. The breath of nostalgia also performs magic.

A friend, call him Victor, decided he was dying. He said his doctor had given him an unfavorable verdict under the illusion that he was wise and tough and deserved the truth. Or perhaps this was just a fantasy Victor enjoyed after less dramatic bouts of frequent urination. In any case, he gassed up the family Volvo, but then bought a Corvette he spotted at a widow's sale and went zigzagging across country, from the east coast to the west, having researched many of the old girlfriends from his busy, devoutly predatory, youthful Casanovaism. (Personally, with his dark good looks and brooding eyes, he thought he was more like Don Juan, cursed with the destiny of pursuing perfect true love. He considered it a Quest.)

He didn't merely register his conquests and carelessly move on. He was a writer. He chronicled them in the stack of journals he had accumulated through the years. He treasured each near-perfect page, poignantly regretting the discovery that the woman of that season was almost, up to a point . . . but then not quite perfect enough. Without tragic disappointment, however, how would his deepest stories be born? Sometimes I didn't think losing a prom queen runner-up to a basketball player qualified as tragedy, but I never disagreed with him when he showed me the resultant tale of disillusion.

There was a flaw in Don Juan's armor. He had married three, then four of the imperfect young women. Now, in later life, he was still married to number four, Claudia, a caregiving sort, with whom he fathered two children. Having committed herself to him, she also took up the word profession. He was a middling successful teacher and writer; she was a hopeful but unpublished poet. "What kind of poetry are you writing?" I asked.

"Experimental poetry," she explained.

Victor growled menacingly: "Means it isn't printed square on the page."

She turned suppliant eyes toward her former professor, present spouse. "I'm working toward getting published, and I'm starting to receive encouraging notes from magazines. *Poetry* asked me to submit again."

"Never submit, *conquer*," Victor said. He quoted one of her shorter poems, waving his arms to indicate the spacing of the lines on the page:

> We don't know nothing.
> About that too much.

"It's a Sicilian saying she picked up someplace, so she thought it would make a haiku about the existence of God. Not having seventeen syllables is part of the meaning. Subtle, right?" He cast his dark eyes heavenward as he recalled the relevant critique from *Much Ado About Nothing*: "Stirs the wind in that corner?"

Claudia had taken a Shakespeare class with him. She wasn't the best student, but she had the most soothing bosom.

I could understand how, even without a fatal tumor growing, if it was, Victor might want to embark on a nostalgic road trip through great, truehearted (Jack Kerouac, Thomas Wolfe) America, stopping in Ithaca, Columbus, Iowa City, and other towns where he stored erotic memories. He would unlock them, he would restore their grandeur. Some of the women were now located in big cities and married; no problem. It would be his first time in Albuquerque.

Find them! Bed them once more! Move right along on the next stop of the terminal sex tour!

Be young again. Write elegiacally in his journal about the lonely hooting of the long freight trains crossing the prairie lands of great, truehearted America (see previous citations) while he pursued the dream of soulful lovemaking with women who were now, like him, in late middle age or later. Most of the cross-prairie traffic at this time in great, truehearted (ibid.) America's history was carried by lonely trucks or lonely aircraft, but that was a mere detail. In his heart the railway hooted.

He telephoned his wife regularly during the Farewell Reprise Sex Recovered & Revised Memory Tour. She understood that he needed this experience for his writing. She was a caregiver, and besides, as an experimental poet, she understood about how permanent in a deep soul temporary loves must be. "Hi, honey, I'm in Kansas City."

"Kansas?"

"No, across the river in Kansas City, Missouri. I knew her when she was at Wellesley, really nice hair. She dyes it now. How're the kids?"

"Gwen has a cough and a runny nose —"

By the time he reached San Francisco, he was both pensive and deeply enthusiastic, reality wrestling against mania. Even in age, the brooding dark eyes, shadowed by deep smudges (late nights, not kidney disease), were still poetic in their baleful gaze. We had been would-bees together in postdivorce Greenwich Village. Now he needed to remove his glasses to fix his eyes on the object under seduction or scrutiny. He had tried contact lenses, but the itch distracted him. Anyway, nearsightedness, farsightedness, and macular degeneration were not moral flaws unless he happened to find himself driving in heavy traffic. He forgave moral flaws easily, since who in this valley of grief can be perfect? His own novels were mostly sad, except for the ones that were hopeless. For his occasional invitations to read on campus, he kept a lucky shirt with a torn elbow — undergraduate women seemed to read the tear as someone who needed their consolation.

"Some of them get older!" he reported. "Some of them don't care! Some of them don't remember!"

I consoled him as best I could. "But you remember."

Abruptly he calmed himself. "I remember. I care." He grinned his old handsome, self-delighted smile. "It's my job. I'll get a book out of this. Maybe I'll call it *Travels with Myself*."

"That's the ticket, Victor."

"And," he said ominously, lowering his voice, "I'll find new memories. There's life in the boy yet. This time I'll make sure they'll never forget me."

"Hey, Victor," I said, "don't be an ax murderer, okay?"

We laughed together, colleagues, old friends. San Francisco was his last stop before heading home to the experimental poet, soon to be published in several journals, and the daughter with a runny nose and touch of bronchitis. Claudia welcomed him back with a nice casserole and mashed potatoes dinner. Home cooked is a treat when a person has been on the road. Later, he could rest on her familiar soft bosom. She wasn't the sharpest wife he'd had, but she was tops in the placidity field. She may have thought her poetry was importantly innovative; forgiveness of her husband's doubts was one of her strong suits. Who cared if the stupid so-called poetry mostly revolutionized the post-Ginsbergian generation by not getting printed square on the page? Devoted cooking, soft bosom, peace in the household.

Some pillows are too soft for best alignment of the spine, also known as the backbone.

Not long after, Victor's driver's license wasn't renewed, due to macular degeneration. If he was writing the epic of his on-the-road recap, he didn't write it; that is, didn't finish it. The terminal illness that had sent him on his quest didn't kill him. It may only have been a polite way of explaining his need to Claudia. But in fact, he died, his love affairs and his books not everlasting in human memory; his death definitely everlasting.

The experimental poet asked a number of his friends to contribute reminiscences of him for the first issue of a magazine she planned to publish, later issues specializing in post-Ginsbergian poetry not printed square on the page. We celebrated him for virtues that came into relief when he was no longer present to insist on the imperative reality of his dreams.

Gwen, the annoying daughter, dropped out of school and ran away with a skinhead at age sixteen. Pregnant, she got a job at a Wal-Mart in Jacksonville, Florida, where she could support her husband until he got a job as a rock star in a heavy metal Aryan Nation band, as soon as he bought a guitar and learned to play it.

Hasn't Changed Since the Senior Prom

Francis Xavier, unhappily but persistently married these many years, needed to confide the rediscovery of his glamorous youth one fateful evening. It was not a dark and stormy night; such weather would be mere melodrama — this was life and Fate. It was also an art gallery opening at Modernism, balmy and springlike in San Francisco, many of the women dressed in black pantssuits, most of the others in form-fitting black frocks. In front of a Mark Stock painting, *The Butler in Love*, stood a rule-defying breaker of all the current prescribed art opening dress codes.

She was wearing an orange top over a black skirt. Her eyes met his across the room, the recognition urgent, immediate. She had been his college senior prom date forty years ago.

"Forty years? You still recognized each other?"

"It was easy," he said proudly. "She hadn't changed one bit."

I did the math. From age approximately twenty-two, she was now age approximately sixty-two. And she hadn't changed one bit. Evidently it had been that one meaningful prom event that kept her preserved as a delicious revenant from the nineteen-sixties. Rediscovered love, retroactive great passion, works miracles, especially for Francis Xavier. "Amazing," I murmured.

He stared meaningfully, mournfully, because they hadn't seen each other in so long, and each had gone through marriages, and now they were both lonely, he married, she widowed . . . It was a beautiful time to re-meet. Fate must have had a hand in it. Prostate surgeries and hysterectomies are not immediately visible at art gallery openings.

Frank's wife dressed like an escapee from *Vogue* (they were rich) forty years ago. She had seen no reason to change her style. He was tired, tired, tired of her. She felt the same way about him. She might have wanted a divorce, but the community property issues . . . much too annoying. He might have wanted a divorce, but he was shy by nature. Also, he didn't know what damage his wife's lawyers might do to his family trust. It would be a happy solution for his wife if she could find a lover, and the thought didn't bother him at all because it was only a thought. When he gazed upon her nose hairs, carelessly untrimmed, he knew a lover wouldn't happen . . . But for him, in general, meeting the miracle lady who hadn't changed one iota in forty years was splendidly serendipitous.

"So now what, Frank?" I asked.

He meditated. The loneliness of an unhappy marriage is worse than the loneliness of widowhood. It was important to explain this fact to Lisa, for that was her name.

"You spoke?"

"I asked if she wanted a drink elsewhere, not just the wine they were serving for the vernissage, red or white, no valid choice. Someplace where we could sit down. The little bar at the Palace, not the Palace Court, but the intimate lounge — you know it?"

"And?"

"She said she was a graduate of A.A."

"Do they graduate?" I reasoned my way through the problem. "But maybe she can drink coffee."

"Um," he said. He hadn't thought of that in the fever of the moment. He leaned toward me and whispered, "But she gave me her cell phone number. I told her she still looks like Edie."

"Who?"

"She also told me I still look the same, too. Edie *Sedgwick.*" He had been an Art History major until he discovered people thought he was gay and changed to French. There was a lot of nostalgia for Andy Warhol still operating. I was sympathetic. The sixties had been fun. But Edie Sedgwick had died very young, the sure way never to change the look.

Paradoxically, the fact that his wife never changed *her* look annoyed him. Her hair had grown frizzy. Her thighs . . . But he didn't want to speak ill of his wife. All he was willing to say was that he really hated her, and the kid was grown up, but still they were stuck.

Although raised by an outspoken mother in Cleveland, I had tried to learn some coastal manners and didn't ask if he was bound to his wife only by estate and community property issues. I looked at this white-haired man with the thinness combed carefully over his patchy spot, his pencil-thin white mustache quivering, and didn't say, "You haven't changed, either."

"Either?" he asked.

So I thought I didn't say it, but actually, I did. I was bemused.

He measured me with care. "You've matured, Herb. You still almost have a spring in your step. Maybe your girlfriends from college might recognize you, if you had one."

"Thanks." And I really didn't say, Sorry about your osteoporosis and the dowager hump and that hair that leaves the pink of your scalp shining so bright a person can read by it . . . And I actually did manage not to say those things.

We cannot be indicted for fraud, nor convicted of a public offense, nor sentenced to anything but sleepless dreaming for lying to ourselves. The complications of love and marriage, child rearing and adventuring, companionship and lust, impulse and loyalty make for extenuating circumstances. The force that throbs through us can be tamed, subdued, closed off. It cannot be denied until the light finally goes out.

I may not really care for Frank, Francis Xavier. But I respect his brave, maybe desperate clinging to a vision. How could I not be sympathetic with another aging man suddenly struck by romance, the memory of romance, the hope of one more love, the great one? How could I not?

I managed somehow. And yet, within the tickle of ridicule — I'm not tangled in his overheated underwear — I know that we are companions on this road. We yearn toward eternity with "the love of my life"; we refuse to admit that this road to eternity eventually comes to a full stop. There was a gleam in the eyes of Francis Xavier, sudden tension in his face, the animal sensing springtime again, one more mating season, blood speeding and that unusual glow. I like gleam. I value glow. I admire them. I'd better have no more scorn for Francis Xavier than I have for myself.

I, too, would prefer to defy mortality and the inevitable. I, too, see myself as I once was, despite the evidence of the mirror and, on occasion, the tendons behind my left knee.

Sexual Perversity in Cleveland

The winds of sixties sexual freedom, sung, danced, bongo'd, and guitar'd about, seem to have left eddies of fifties marital togetherness in idyllic corners of the universe, such as my hometown, Cleveland, the Paris of Northeastern Ohio. My childhood friend Harold, lucky enough to marry his high school sweetie and remain in Cleveland as a college teacher, came to visit San Francisco, courtesy of an academic convention.

The subject under review at our dinner was intended to be nostalgia about a shared past, but instead it turned out to be his present exciting erotic adventure. He had met a woman! A fellow teacher at the convention! Incendiary eyes met, and it was clear they both wanted the same thing!

Since they were staying at the Hilton, their affair required no travel other than a short, breathless elevator ride. "How was it?" I asked.

"Oh, man."

This was powerful stuff, this was real, it was no one-night stand — they could spend three nights together at the Hilton Hotel in the glamorous cool gray city of love. "We could have!" he cried, shreds of California summer squash flying from his mouth.

"Could have what?" The sweat of desire and summer squash with olive oil on the upper lip, plus the gleam of passion over his entire face, brightened our meal. His paper on "The Importance of Period Furniture in Henry James' *The Spoils of Poynton*" had generated probing questions from many, and meaningful eye contact with one.

But something here confused me. "You said *could have?*"

My old friend was boiling with joy. He couldn't wait to get home to Beatrice, his wife. "That colleague from Denver was so . . . we didn't do anything."

"What?"

"Well, if we did, I'd have to tell Beatrice."

? ? ? ? stated my entire upper body.

"We tell each other everything," he explained.

I was bewildered. "So since you tell each other everything, you're going to tell Bea how you had this fantastic passion for the delicious woman from Denver, and she did too, and you could have, but you didn't? You'll map out the whole scene?"

"Oh, boy. The seminar, the cash bar off the lounge area . . . we sat in a corner, and her knees, I could feel the heat —"

Explanation relieved neither my confusion nor my sympathy for Beatrice, a woman I've always admired. She had written most of the dissertation Harold needed for his graduate degree. "How do you think she'll feel," I asked, "after you map out the Hilton, the eye contact, the hot knees, what you both wanted, your knees touching in the dark, leading up to nothing?"

"Oh, Herb, she'll be so proud of me."

"Togetherness," a slogan of *The Saturday Evening Post* in the fifties, still reigns in secret gardens of America. It was an ideal of Norman Rockwell–illustrated family unity, aiming toward a loyal subscriber base, although eventually the magazine went out of business anyway. This was also the time in Cleveland, Toledo, Detroit, and Buffalo when driving a foreign automobile could earn a drastic keying in patriotic parking lots. Although Alan Freed, a Cleveland radio disc jockey, had brought raunchy "race music" out of a segregated scene into what became the mainstream, pronounced like one word, "rocknroll," much of my blessed hometown may cling to older verities.

I am a stubborn and willful eldest son of an eldest son. I glared at Harold. "You could have, but you didn't, and now you'll tell Bea all about it and you expect her to be happy?"

He was still flushed and excited. He loved San Francisco. "Yes! Very very proud! I phoned her and told her I have a surprise for her and she said it better be good because why didn't I use a phone card for a long distance call?"

Having prepared his confession, anticipated his wife's reward, Harold calmed down. "You know, Herb, we have zucchini just as good in our city of Cleveland, but we cook it in butter, not this Italian olive oil they seem to like around here."

"Harold! This is California summer squash," I said.

The Eternal Rekindling

A nationwide expedition in search of lost, past, and therefore eternal beloveds — rescuing his glamorous history, redeeming the debris of romantic stabs in the dark — was just the ticket for Victor, campus heartbreaker emeritus. His own lyrical temperament was an underappreciated national treasure. He felt deep sympathy for himself. He bade a fond unregretful farewell to his family, roared away from home in the vintage Corvette bought for this purpose, headed crosscountry to bask in the aura of every departed girlfriend he could find. Thanks to his research skills, he found many. His wife, one of his former students, understood that this was a thing he really, really, really needed to do; he was a champion explainer, she was a champion explainee. Perhaps she also could do with a rest.

It could be recorded as the Super Geriatric Sex Tour Epic. He believed he was dying (isn't everybody?), and it was incumbent on Victor, champion romantic, to check in once more. Did Miss Poughkeepsie treasure the memory of him as he did of her, at least until he moved right along on the Interstate to Miss Cincinnati? Who was also unique in her own twangy Appalachian way?

Some of those now grown-up women shrugged, assented, spent a nostalgic hour or two between the clean sheets of his hotel rooms. Fulfillment brought irritation, impatience in some cases, but the ensemble of the experience, the gestalt, was satisfactory because he also shared warmhearted dinners with amused former lovers who touched his hand and offered a hug before sending him on his way. ("Sorry, Victor, but thanks for asking.") Best of all, of course, were the women he couldn't find because they had disappeared or managed to hide from him. They were the really perfect ones.

A poetic swain again, Victor sat with me in San Francisco, recounting, eyes swarming with emotion. I wondered if it helped him to tell all while my wife sat with her hands folded in her lap, smiling indulgently. Occasionally his glance darted toward her, waiting for her to go to the kitchen or the bedside of one of our children, so that, man to man, he could specify certain physical details from this voyage of reexploration.

Then he returned home. The dream of perfect love was quelled, surely to rise again, and perhaps it might have. The Corvette held up nicely, except for a bit of transmission trouble in Iowa City.

During his last years, Victor discovered gardening. Fresh air and stoop labor removed him from himself while he worked in muddy boots, cotton gloves, aching back. There were tomatoes until the first frost. Mulch. Smells of leaves returning to the elements of earth, not irksome like old loves. The smells were strong, sharp, rich, penetrating his diminished olfactory talents. His diminished sense of smell, he confessed, was also irksome. Mulch, rotting leaves, tomato vines with the faint acidity of the fruit were reassuring because loss of the sense of smell was a sign of Alzheimer's, which he dreaded. He could still smell mulch, rotting leaves, fallen bird-scarred tomatoes. Nature, the agrarian life, was another way of tuning in the universe, a tradition like sex with students. "Otherwise," he wrote, "all I'd have is the smell of my own shit, and that isn't good enough." He told me not to worry if he repeated himself; it was only for emphasis.

His daughter, Gwen, silent, withdrawn, tattooed, dressing in Goth black, departed the family, but at least she didn't commit suicide, not yet. Anorexia . . . well, maybe her pregnancy would cure that. Victor was hanging tough.

He kept in touch with me as a treasured witness of his

history and his cross-country quest. I could almost smell the frosted tomato vines when he telephoned late one night: "Sometimes I think it was all an imaginary solution to a problem that didn't exist, what do you think?

"Don't get mellow on me, Victor."

But the real point of the call was to let me know that despite his late-life commitment to Claudia and the garden, both his acuity and his sense of humor, or irony, as he preferred to call it, were still present and accounted for. "I'm keeping dementia at bay, pal, and may you do the same."

"Thanks for the good wishes."

He asked if he reminded me of that knight who went in search of the Holy Grail. "What's his name, Herb?"

"I'll look it up."

"Galahad, man. Parsifal in that opera by what's-his-face. Ha-ha, I remember, you don't."

"I'll start a garden tomorrow, Victor. Do you know what time it is in San Francisco?"

"Oh, sorry, I woke you up? But this was important."

Claudia's soft bosom was a constant. After a morning of writing, an afternoon of gardening, an evening of quarreling with the remaining daughter, he helped Claudia make a nice fire in the fireplace before they tucked in. Starlight, leaves falling, ripening night, the telephone ringer turned off.

"And how are you?" he asked. "Got anything going for yourself?"

We sleep and sleep. We sleep through childhood, youth, our adult lives. We sleep after lovemaking. We sleep in depression, or if we can't, we seek to sleep. We sleep fitfully in old age.

For most of us, the largest single part of the day is spent in sleep. We don't usually interrupt sleep to eat or clean the house or work on taxes; if we do, we wish we hadn't. We hope to restore the body and spirit in sleep. Dreams are essential. We sleep to dream.

Dreams also nourish or infect the part of our lives that's not sleep. Victor and Francis Xavier needed their dreams, just as all of us need our dreams carried over as reward or punishment from sleep. Love is a most persistent dream. Sometimes it turns toward nightmare.

Francis Xavier liked to quote one of Yeats's late poems: "When the mouth dies, what is there?" In a youthful male, a look across the room tends to make the man into a striding-across machine, uttering some variation on the mating bray: "So, do you come here often?" "Don't I know you from someplace?" The aging male can be a machine for turning the look across the room into redemption of an entire existence.

Francis Xavier remembered the woman across the gallery from their senior prom. The heart is full of longing; the heart is full of regret; why did he marry someone else? Francis Xavier's congested heart now sought a period of delusion. My friend Ed Pols (real name) loved, trusted, treasured, lived in solidarity with Eileen, his wife. Harold (not his real name) leaned precariously in the world, leaned against his wife, needing maternal care. After much practice over the years, he didn't really yearn for anything else, but thought he should.

Aging is perplexing to most of those who get there. We recall our youth, yesterday it was, and wonder, How did I get here? Wasn't I supposed to conquer inevitability? You mean the laws of nature apply to me, too?

While evolving toward brotherly feeling for Francis Xavier, even toward Victor and his enraged quest for departed love in all four directions and perhaps the fifth dimension, too, Harold, the romantic swain from Cleveland, presents a challenge. I feel sympathy for his wife, although she must have chosen what she has — this husband, this spouse, this Harold. Generosity toward Harold glows fitfully. I breathe on the embers and they go out. Alas, help me, please, saintliness has fallen from my soul.

The ungainly old romantics like Victor, Francis Xavier, even Harold, surely are owed my forgiveness because I'm also laughable. Love goes where it wants; we're helpless as it carries us along. We must want to be helpless, haunted by true or false events of love. This shouldn't be a surprise. Two people are involved, after all — two who remain mysteries to each other while they cleave together as if they are one. But if the mouth dies, what is there? Why turn to stone before returning to dust?

Victor, Francis Xavier, and Harold aspired toward perfect love, just short of the perfect and eternal love found by the Norwegian captain and his wife in Jacmel, Haiti. Not immune to their condition, it's an arrogance to suggest forgiveness of my old friends' delusions and excesses. I *must* forgive them, O Aphrodite, for I, too, am a sinner.

Almost everyone remembers glimpsing his or her perfect completion, the dream lover, the soul mate, at a traffic light or sitting in a train speeding in the opposite direction or passing in a crowd when eyes meet for an instant. One sleepless night, jet-lagged in a Manhattan August, a stifling heat wave August, I fled from the Hotel Chelsea, wanting better turmoil than the one I was suffering in a strange bed. Calling for air-conditioning repair would not have helped. It was at that three A.M. which has been celebrated as the soul's darkest hour and the loneliest, with or without the buzz of ventilation. I found an all-night diner on West Twenty-third Street and thought: Scrambled eggs and coffee, that's the ticket, what the hell, let's pretend it's breakfast time.

Among nightshift workers, speed freaks, pimps, hookers of many sexes and permutations — and ordinary distressed citizens like me — I felt more at home, nourished by company even before my eggs arrived. There was a pair of cops at the counter, shedding powdered sugar and flecks of glaze from their police-procedural donuts. Fried grease is essential to shape up the belly and belt from which equipment hangs. They dunked — maybe that's also the rule. Their rumps flowed over the stools. They were talking to each other in low voices. Although my hearing was still sharp — that's how long ago it was — I couldn't make out what they were saying, but gave myself a paranoia quiz: No, they weren't talking about me or my marriage. A whine of fluorescence overhead; the jukebox stood illuminated, waiting, but silent; blasts of cold air. I unfolded the early edition of *The New York Times*.

Destiny then pulled one of its sly tricks on a night wanderer who had set out only in search of air-conditioning, protein, caffeine, and distraction from *le cafard*, the cockroach blues. A young woman was sitting in a stained mahogany-colored vinyl booth a few stained mahogany-colored vinyl booths ahead of my own. She was writing in a spiral note-book; her hair was tawny and thick; her mug of coffee stood unattended, probably cold. She didn't look up. I also carried a notebook in my pocket, pulled it out, pushed the newspaper aside. I poised my pen over a blank page. The page remained blank. I had nothing to write. I thought of sketching her. Her lips were pressed together in concentration and her own ballpoint moved swiftly. I neither wrote nor sketched.

Finally I wrote: *Not yet four o'clock. Won't be dawn for an hour or so. There's a person . . .* When I looked up, she was standing, dropping money on the table, and heading out into the glowing, steaming, middle-of-the night August Manhattan street.

In our culture, especially with a couple of nourished NYPD cops nearby, it would have been inadvisable for me to leap up, follow her, and inquire if she happened to know the interesting French word *cafard*. Which is probably why, many years later, I'm still following her.

Tawny hair, thick and careless at this hour, the smudged eyes of a night person, an insomniac or an inspired poet with erroneous skin, sallow, her pen speeding over the pages of a spiral notebook . . . Not much to go on, but I've gone over it for thirty-five years now. My wife and I had just parted in San Francisco, I was thinking about how to pick up the pieces at midlife, I never again saw the young woman with the tawny, thick, careless hair. Maybe she was a crazy, maybe she was merely a normal occasional insomniac, maybe she had also just parted from a husband or a lover, maybe she had no fear of late-night Manhattan streets, maybe she and I would have loved each other forever.

Well, no, that was unlikely. But we never quarreled, did

we? Right there, that's enough evidence for a perfect, unfailing, undying love.

I offer this incident in my disfavor to prove that I'm as foolish about love in my way as Victor, Francis Xavier, and Harold in theirs. Since I've changed their names to conceal their shame; perhaps I should change mine, too. But what's the use? The dream of perfect love is a blessed affliction. It was for them; it is for me; and it can make us as foolish in age as we were in youth. It also offers proof that we're still alive and the blood stirring. It stirs still, especially during certain sleepless nights when there is no body by our side, or the body that is there is ninety-eight point six degrees cold.

Foolish and dreamy men (boys) took love from where it used to be, before marriage and romance, to where it is now. This might have been the end of it, except that foolish and dreamy women (women) tugged and urged and conspired with men to make the whole thing as complicated as it will never stop being. Flawed aptitude for love is a normal pre-existing condition in human nature. Since the aptitude is precious, we'll have to live with the flaws.

7

King of the Cleveland Beatniks

I believed from childhood on that part of my job in life was to be a proper big brother to Sid. We escaped the neighbor boy in Lakewood together, but there were demons that Sid never found a way to evade.

He is years gone now and the novel he spent nearly fifty years writing, never finished, sits in four sagging boxes in my bedroom. I try and keep trying to read it. I carry a crate out into a sunny room, take out a handful of paper, admire some of the sentences and paragraphs, and can't go on. I follow a story until it stops without coming to an end and then start another story. There is a search going on here, a sadness, explosions of wrath and fantasy, and then an abrupt halt, sometimes in the middle of a sentence. I put the papers back in the box and carry it to my bedroom.

"Sid passed." For a moment I thought our brother Bob in Cleveland was calling me in San Francisco to tell me Sid had taken a driving test.

"What?"

He repeated the words and I was irritated by the language. Bob had telephoned Sid for three days, he didn't answer the phone, and finally Bob went to his apartment. His car was in the parking lot; he had to be there. The custodian wouldn't open the door until they called the police. They found him sitting in the bathroom, and Bob said, "Why don't you answer the phone?" The cop took his arm, held it, and said, "Because he's dead."

He was the kid brother I bullied, nagged, and loved, the one who remembered the childhood we shared. He was the one I took long confiding walks with. We became restless boys again in our hometown, or sometimes in San Francisco, and even in Paris the one time I managed to persuade him to use his passport.

He tended to stay with his uncompleted business in Cleveland, but he kept a passport ready and travel plans in the works. First, though, there were things he had to do. He wanted to spend more time with my children and me as soon as he finished his novel. When The Novel would be finished, just a little organization needed, pretty soon, maybe a whole completed section ready by the next time we talked; then it would be great to take it easy, go on a trip, relax with folks who had preceded him in the very interesting techniques of just enjoying life . . . I keep nearby the boxes of manuscripts, notebooks, clippings, three-by-five cards, menus with scribbled phrases, scraps. He started writing The Novel during the part of one year he spent at Ohio State University, during most of which he kept busy riding a motorcycle, writing his novel, and not going to class. In a journal in a loose-leaf notebook, he wrote that the dean who expelled him informed him that he had the ability to do college-level work at OSU, but that it was a requirement for freshmen students that they occasionally attend class, show up for exams, write assigned papers. Sid understood perfectly and thanked the dean for his invitation to return at some future date.

He spent the next three years keeping busy not communicating with anyone in his family. Dead silence. From hints before he left, hitchhiking out of Cleveland with a cardboard suitcase, I had an idea of where he was, working in carnivals traveling the southern circuit, running a midway game called the count store, thinking about his novel. As a seventeen-year-old, I had hitchhiked out of town, taking the same suitcase, and attached myself to southern road shows. After trying to wait him out, I used an occasion to put an advertisement in *Billboard*, saying: Sid, I'm getting married, I want you to meet my wife.

He reappeared, weathered and tan, bringing gifts of Pendleton shirts and an Indian blanket. "Sid, what have you been doing?"

"Writing my novel."

"You should have let us know where you were, Sid."

"I was gonna."

When he died, he had been writing his novel for fifty years. I keep watch over the four cardboard boxes filled with it. He was gonna finish it and let the world know where on earth he had been.

Talkative, companionable, but with a gleamy opaqueness behind his glasses when he was orating at table, emitting ropy streams of opinion, reminiscence, fiats about politics, religion, health food — whatever engaged his attention — he gathered followers to listen and pass the time at Arabica, the café where he held court. He sat at the center of a group in Cleveland who knew that they really belonged on the road or encamped in a dramatic outpost of Bohemia. Ibiza maybe, or perhaps Bali. They were only temporarily in Cleveland because of the convenience of picking up the welfare check, or they had a family who demanded attendance for dinner on national or religious holidays, or their A.A. group decided they weren't ready to travel just yet. This didn't mean they weren't explorers in the farthest expanse of the bohemian archipelago. Little-known fact: Cleveland embodies the Left Bank, North Beach, any of the new or old Greenwich Villages, just as Walt Whitman contained multitudes. Hart Crane and R. Crumb had lived in Cleveland before the Arabica bohemians, and they were pioneers for those who would surely follow after.

Sid was a sovereign in this democracy of wish. His novel was on the verge of finding its shape tomorrow or next month or soon. In the meantime, to rest from his expectations, he took on all comers at chess.

The King of the Cleveland Beatniks ruled gently, although after he stopped playing for money, he became a killer at the chessboard. Chess moves were no mystery to him; since it was only a game, rashness and impatience were allowed in Cleveland. Sid preferred presiding to ruling. He sat with coffee, nervous hands, and patchy beard over his table at Arabica. His friends gave deference, laughed among themselves at his repetitions, enjoyed his stories, liked the way his stories expanded and evolved in the repeating, cared for him. He was their guy. Once, visiting Cleveland, I heard him tell a newcomer to his table that he was "semi-retired," and while I thought, *Semi from what?* one of his friends called him sharply to order: "Sid! Your novel! You're working on it."

In a dusty apartment in an anonymous apartment block, alone, needing help, he was found half-sitting among the blood heaved up in an explosion from his heart. The apartment was dusty because he didn't clean it much and didn't want other people to come to clean, either. They might disturb his manuscripts, the long narrative that wound like a snake through the years of his life.

"Let me see some of it," I would ask on my visits to Cleveland or when he visited me in San Francisco.

"Next time," he would say. "Next time, I promise. I've just got to pull some things together."

"Let me see a few pages. Sometimes a reader helps."

"It's going good. I want to get it organized first, Herb."

"When?"

"I'll send it to you. I've got the mailing envelopes already. It just needs a little more work."

He worked as a cabdriver, as caretaker of a laundromat, and in a Ford factory. As a cabdriver, didn't like the scams of hookers, johns, and pimps; as a laundromat operator, got bored with the smell of detergent, left the place in a buddy's charge, went off to drink coffee and make notes; as an autoworker, left his paychecks in his pants until they expired (in the meantime, had no money). For a while, he ran a poker game. That worked okay; he took his share of the pot, gave advice, bought sandwiches, and made instant coffee. During the years traveling through the south in a carnival, he wanted no contact at all with anyone back home, wherever home was for him. Later he said he planned to write or call, but it just got away from him. He postponed. He was just gonna do it, maybe tomorrow.

When I married, I put that advertisement in *Billboard*, in the Traveling Show issue, asking in capital letters for MY BROTHER SID GOLD to come meet my wife. Maybe he hunkered down in a boardinghouse near Tuscaloosa, Alabama, for some relaxing reading of classified ads; maybe someone said, "Hey Sid, that you?" It must have been the right time for him to leave his silence, this perturbed abstention. Along with the Pendleton shirts and the Indian blanket, he brought stories about sheriffs, gypsies, addicts, a down-home American foreign legion. We talked about the midway, about carny life and language, the interrogatory that went: "Are you with it? . . . With it and for it." I was sure he was planning to write about it. "Naw," he said. "You do it, Herb. I got something else in mind."

I wrote a novel, *The Man Who Was Not With It*, which I dedicated to him. I thought the book was fantasy, my own dream of wandering and escape, built out of the carnival of my adolescent dreams, but a review in *Billboard* accused me of giving away the secrets of the midway, and words I made up appeared in glossaries of carny argot.

Sid explained that this was because carny folks didn't know what was real and what was their dream. "Their world is made of sawdust and smoke, Herb. The same for me. Like it is for me, Herb."

That's why he was writing something else, he said, something that wasn't sawdust and smoke. It would be ready soon.

"What is it?"

He blinked behind his glasses. He drew on his pipe — he'd given up cigarettes because any fool knew they were bad for the health, but he inhaled deeply from his pipe. He could tell me this much about his novel: I shouldn't crowd him; he was writing about the radical splinter movements of the thirties. He was interested in the Schachtmanites and the Lovestoneites (Trotsky was too mainstream for him). He was writing about the dark poor of the Depression. There was a Croatian coal miner in Appalachia, a man who had run away from a city slum. He and his friends lived without women in rural boardinghouses and sent money home. "It's complicated, Herb, but I'm putting it together."

In the late fifties, when he was broke as usual, just fired from one of his jobs, I wrestled a story away from him, a tale about a stubborn thief in jail at Christmastime, and it was printed in one of the *Playboy* imitations of the time. There was a dreamy longing for love in it, and the editor of *Nugget* (or was it *Dude* or *Gent*?) had a sentimental streak. It appeared in the December issue with a collection of nude girls next door under mistletoe or wrapped in red ribbon. Opposite his story, a cutie, naked except for roller skates and some discreet fifties airbrushing, was pursued by a panting Santa. By the time Sid was holding court at Arabica for the beatniks of Cleveland, the roller skater was probably a grandmother. The story of the lonely thief during the season of celebration is his only published work.

I told him it was a good story. It had his devotion to adventure, and in the pain of a soul behind bars in a small-town jail (was it in Georgia or Alabama?) at that holiday season, which haunts everyone for different reasons, it gave a sense of the general isolation. He wondered what those who bought the magazine for the roller-skating cuties would make of his story, and I delivered a little lecture about the ways of commerce, the need of men's magazines to avoid trouble with their mailing privileges, and assured him that the editor of *Nugget* (or *Dude* or *Gent*) really valued literature above everything except his job and staying clear of federal, state, or local obscenity experts. "That's not what writing is about," he said.

Agreed, and he shouldn't have to think about it. So I told him I could help him find an agent.

"Naw," he said. "That's not what I want to write. As soon as I get the novel together, you'd like to read it, wouldn't you?"

"Let me see what you've got."

"Good idea. Right, right. Pretty soon, Herb."

Over the years I expressed my exasperation with his floating, postponing, late-sleeping life by criticizing his language, as if a better explanation would resolve matters. When I telephoned, he would say, "I was just gonna write to you, Herb," or "I was just gonna send you part of my novel," or "I was just gonna call you." I told him he had invented a new grammatical form, the Future Conditional Imperative Subjunctive, the I-was-just-gonna.

I knew he was staring, perturbed and gray, squinting behind his thick glasses, needing to clip his beard. His face was permanently furrowed with worry. "I'm gonna finish a section of my book this weekend. Next time I see you, I'll show it to you."

"Why don't you send it to me?"

"Yeah. Yeah, I'll do that, good idea. I was just gonna say that's a good idea."

As soon as his allergies let up . . . as soon as he got through his dental appointments . . . as soon as he finished some research about glaucoma he was doing in the library . . .

as soon as he could get it typed more neatly . . ."Good idea, Herb. Yes, I want you to read it. I'm working on it every day."

As children, we slept in twin beds in the same room. We took turns telling stories to each other at night, the usual ones — flying over houses to escape monsters, swimming under seas to find lost continents, battling in jungles for justice or for our lives. When we were told by our mother to be quiet, tomorrow was a school day, we continued in whispers. I frightened him or he frightened me, and then we faded into the miracle of sleep, continuing our adventures without companionship because that's the way the world often was.

This busy dreaming may have set us permanently into the storytelling mode. Although the stories go on and on, some find ways to end them and he never did. His dreams wandered the skies and swam the seas and gazed at monsters and never reached a state of mere meditation upon the partial wholeness of the world. That acceptance of shapely incompleteness is the paradox of finishing. For him, nothing ever finished.

I remembered something of the spirit of our sleepy adventures when it came time to tell stories for my children. They also liked to walk with him and listen to his ramble, his explorations, his far-fetched dartings into anecdote and fabulous inventions, sometimes ending in bursts of unexpected laughter. They made links where he made none, or perhaps they didn't need links, since the adventures were exotic and his grin was reassuring. "Did that really happen to you, Uncle Sid?"

"What do you think?"

"Well, maybe . . ."

"So that's why I'm telling you." And they preferred that it did happen; the sea lion must really have carried him under the ice, it was much better to think so.

Among his papers were photographs, faded brown, of the two of us in short pants, probably three and four years old, sitting proud in a cart pulled by a goat. In our hearts we were fighter pilots, or perhaps fighter goat riders. I am holding the reins. Surely both our mother and the proprietor of the goat and the cart are standing nearby, begging these solemn boys to smile. But we have our own intentions, we don't smile. This is our serious business, too important for us to waste energy listening to a mother and a gypsy with a goat. I'm sure Sid wants to hold the reins. I'm not sure if I let him.

Our youngest brother, calling with the news, had cleared his throat and said: "Sid passed." Something mysterious had happened, and I hated that he was telephoning from Cleveland to pronounce this verb without a direct object. I was irritated by the language, but maybe *passed* was the right word anyway. It's familiar habit in families — the words "familiar" and "family" are close relatives and often as troublesome with each other as close relatives are — to fall into patterns of vexation.

When our mother caught us fighting (translation: I was beating Sid up), she reached for the telephone and asked for the police department. "Hello, Officer Cecil? I have a very bad boy here." Next I would be going to jail, and it would serve me right. I folded my arms and looked my best hardened criminal, waiting for the swift chariot of justice to carry me away, but Sid begged piteously, "Don't, don't, we were only playing."

"Playing? Playing? You call that playing?"

"Herb was showing me how to wrestle."

"*Boxing*," I muttered. "Didn't grab him by the neck."

"Just a second, Officer Cecil." She paused, the telephone in her hand. "Promise you'll stop with the funny business?"

While I stood there, arms still folded in defiant miscreant mode, Sid said, tears streaming, "Yes, we promise — please?"

"Officer Cecil? I think we may be able to deal with this." Reluctantly she replaced the receiver.

But then soon enough I was again pushing him around, this time because he wanted to play with my friends and me and didn't he understand that he was nearly two years younger and ineligible for our big guy baseball? He deserved a lesson, but again it was interrupted by our mother with the telephone. "Okay, that's it, now you go," she said, and I arrived at an early poker move. I reached for the phone and said, "Mom, you're tired, let me call for you."

She stood there, stymied, and muttered something about our father coming home with a big fist to drive some sense into my head. When she disappeared, Sid and I stood giggling together, and then I grandly spoke up for him as a right fielder on my team. We had been afforded an early preview of adult life in the category entitled Calling the Bluff. While sharing my knowledge with him, I basked in his admiration and told him he could put Officer Cecil in his story that night. I felt emotions related to gratitude, brotherly love, even sympathy — complexities of feeling due, with luck, to come later — and never shoved, poked, hit, or tackled him again. Except maybe during neighborhood football, and then only because he was clumsy and fumbled easy passes. He was my brother, and I wanted him to view matters as they were, learn coordination. Officer Cecil became our secret friend.

Years later, when I fled to Sid for comfort, and I did, it was because of trouble in a marriage. When family shipwrecks, a welcome from family is salvation for a drowning man. He listened to me as I repeated the helpful nonsense of a surgeon friend who said, "Cut off a leg and it's gone forever. But psychological pain doesn't last." He knew better than most that this is helpful and untrue. It lasts. He walked with me; he listened to my troubles until they repeated themselves into postmarital whining, as repeated pain does; we went to all-night movies together; I slept on his couch, my head buried in a tufted mohair Goodwill pillow.

"It's okay, Herb," he said, "it's okay." Since we were brothers, I understood him. It was not okay, we both knew it was not okay, but Sid and Herb would always be brothers and that could be counted on. For a while, I gave up judgment of him — all the judgment I had in stock was turned against myself. I told him thanks and his lips moved, murmuring like a soothing parent. I wrapped myself in an overcoat and sank into the dusty couch.

In later years, we went for long rambles in the neighborhood where we had lived as children — here was the Homestead Theater, remember the candy store over there, let's have lunch in this diner. I said we ought to order meat loaf, mashed potatoes, and fruit Jell-o to cure the nostalgia disease. But for me there was another intention in these trips to Cleveland and these walks. I tried to tell him I was grateful to him for being my brother. I could release for a time the older-brother advice, urgings, nagging, which so often seized me like a tic. I apologized for my bad older-brother habits. "It's okay, Herb," he would say, embarrassed. I told him it was fun to explore the world, the exotic terrains of Cleveland, and let's do more of it, even elsewhere. "Right, right, Herb."

"When?"

One time he managed to work things out, get his novel temporarily in order, date this completion by putting a sheet of newspaper — one of his geological layers — over the pile on a long plank table. He felt free to take a vacation. He had never been out of the country. He applied for a passport, he read some guidebooks, he navigated airline reservations, and although the process was exhausting, he managed to meet me in Paris. I urged him to stay on a few days after I left. He had survived for three years in traveling carnivals, hadn't he? Yes, but that was different, now the novel needed attention, he had some new ideas; time to get back to Cleveland. "Won't it wait a few days?" I asked.

"I had a good time. This was enough," he said. "There's a couple things I want to get down just right."

On his last visit to San Francisco, we went for a hike in the Marin headlands. He was amazed by my sons, who were scrambling off the path and down into gulleys to pick up the litter left by careless campers, gathering junk in their arms to carry it out to the trash cans. "I don't think in Cleveland . . ." he said. "In California, do people do this sort of thing a lot?" He was flushed with pleasure, obliterating the peculiar grayness of recent years. He didn't know what an uncle does, but he liked doing it. Hiking here again the next time, great, great, a great thing to do; for sure next time, soon, Herb.

Instead, he died. Amnesty International and my children were his heirs.

In Cleveland, at the memorial ceremony, I found that this man who lived alone, seemed so lonely, had a life filled with companionship. The king of the Cleveland beatniks had held court daily at his table in Arabica. A chess player, a genial loafer, a pronouncer of verdicts, a man with ambitions, he hung with those who were like him. Single mothers and rock band roadies, crazed stock market and racetrack fanatics, guys with surefire systems and those who knew how to work other people's systems to get various kinds of public assistance, genial easers who pretended to be psychologically disabled but really were, they were his colleagues through the vicissitudes. Sid counseled them on how to trade their food stamps for necessities, if cigarettes happened to be a necessity; how to avoid the fines for overdue books or tapes at the public library; how to duck the hassles.

I should have remembered that he knew his way around. On one of my visits to Cleveland, he took me to a karmic health, organic, all-natural, New Age, vegetarian restaurant, which noted on its calligraphic menu that due to a temporary difficulty in finding organic peas, they were serving Libby's canned peas. Similar problems affected the bean, spinach, and beet crops; oh well. "It's just like San Francisco, right, Herb? Do you have Libby's peas in San Francisco?" This was the Cleveland I loved and left. "Give peas a chance, Herb. You heard that one in San Francisco?" But he also showed me the world's largest used book warehouse (maybe it wasn't) and a Slovakian family-style restaurant where I asked him not to sop up the gravy with his bread. "Why, Herb? This is ethnic gravy."

"It's pork fat melted with flour and sugar."

"Oh. I thought it was healthy ethnic gravy, like macro-biotic."

"Health*ful*," I said. "And it isn't."

My kid brother, the closest to me. That older brother–kid brother unequal tug-of-war altered as we traveled through boyhood, youth, middle age, on the road to our shared inevitable destination; the rules of the play were also set down. For years I nagged him and finally resolved to stop asking to see The Novel. I managed to carry out my resolution. It ate at both of us when I brought it up; anger rose in me, hurt rose in him, when I would say, "Okay, just a piece of it, feedback helps. Okay, just a few pages. It doesn't have to be retyped."

"Pretty soon, Herb. Next time I see you. Right now my allergies are bothering me."

So finally I stopped. He seemed to miss my asking; I wasn't playing by the rules, so he brought it up himself, he would tell me anyway. "I'm having trouble organizing. The story keeps changing. I got a good story going, but . . . I've got it in geological layers."

"Geological layers?"

"What I do, my plan of action, when I finish a section and it starts to take off in another direction, is I spread the *Plain Dealer* for that day over that section — I pick up the paper in the morning at Arabica — so I know when I finished that section, just when it was, a way of keeping things straight, and then I put the next section on top of that, and then when it's done or maybe I'm temporarily stuck, I spread a sheet of paper over that one. It's good to have a system like that, what do you think, Herb? I get going at Arabica, a couple cups of coffee, the *Plain Dealer*, what a rotten newspaper —"

But there's the date at the top of the page. So when he looked back, he would know when, what year, what day, he stopped, completed, or gave up on a certain line of narrative, sheaf of paper. Later, when his allergies let up, or he finished with some dental work, or this holiday season was over and he felt better, he would get back to it. Finish the section, organize the story, make sure everything was tidy and clear.

It seemed that he never looked back. He carried the feeling in his head, but he didn't reread the geological layers. That would only add to the confusion. The important thing was to keep the line going until it came time to organize it, because organization is important, too. Pretty soon. But when I went to gather up the mass of manuscript, the piles on the long plank table, and the other piles transferred to the floor near his closet, there was dust undisturbed, probably the source of his allergies, and some of the deeper geological layers, written on rough copy paper years ago, were crumbling with the infections of coffee spills, tobacco stains, ants, time passing. I read headlines in the *Plain Dealer* about Sputnik, Cuba, Viet Nam, and the hair of a mayor of Cleveland that caught fire over a birthday cake.

Sid was the boy that his parents and his older brother tried to push into getting organized, getting an education, getting a job, getting his life in order. ("What're you, a baby?" our mother asked. "So stop dreaming," our father commanded. "Sid, you've got to start something and then keep at it, little by little, one step at a time," said the older brother, thinking he was more helpful than parents; he wasn't.) One afternoon on a visit to Cleveland, I went to his apartment to wake him, and he made instant coffee, served in jelly glasses, probably because the cups and other glasses were dirty. He stood stirring the coffee and I resisted saying, Hey, it's dissolved. Somehow he got to talking about the wish to have a wife, a family, a body of work. "You come back here, Herb, and we walk around a lot, go to movies, it's like we're kids again. Then you go back to San Francisco —"

He lifted a glass of coffee to his mouth and winced and I thought he had burned himself. But his face was wet with tears. We were raised in the Midwest, in regular-folks America, where men did not weep (they may have been learning lately). I was startled and confused. My own throat was congested. It was not because of the dust in the room, our family allergies. His eyes suddenly swollen, he squinted at me, struggled to compose himself, and said, "Don't feel sorry for me, Herb. These are only selfish tears, Herb."

I was watching a silent earthquake convulse my brother's face. I had seen him cry as a child oppressed by family, by our parents, by me. I had seen him skin his knees and cry. But not since he was ten years old, while I was still saying, "Hey. Hey, watch it there," when, in my bullying opinion at age twelve, he was doing or not doing whatever he should not have been or should have been doing.

Now he was an old man with a shaggy beatnik beard; the King of the Cleveland Beatniks, who had been memorialized in a comic strip by his friend R. Crumb. It was a beatnik beard flecked in gray, a face sallow and lined, the eyes pressed shut behind thick glasses, the boy he still seemed to me demanding that no attention be paid because these were only selfish tears.

I reached for him and he pulled away.

I wanted to end the long habit of apologies, which he seemed to reserve for me. I had often watched him speak angrily, contemptuously, sarcastically about large, abstract, international matters or local air pollution from what he called "the smokeless foundries that blacken the sky." With me, he adopted a style of agreeable cajoling when he was not launched into a theory or the history of something. I liked it best when he sat back and recalled adventures, his telling often funny or sharp as he riffed around the point. Sometimes he just stopped or went past the end or people impatiently stopped him before he got there. He unraveled his stories in a slightly raised voice, worried that people had given up listening. At Arabica he usually had a rapt audience, seeking distraction. Sometimes they tired of listening, but he went on anyway — it didn't make much difference. He wasn't skilled at measuring his audience. At family dinners, our mother, still shrewd and bossy at age ninety, would say, "Sid, enough already, we're eating."

He looked startled and paused for the inevitable: "Sid, you're dropping your food. It goes from the fork to the mouth, no side trips."

He would swipe at the table with his napkin.

Now the older cohort was gone and the boy was crying and I reached for him. In the Midwest, in our suburb of Cleveland, brothers don't do that. He pulled away and said sharply, almost commandingly: "No! Selfish tears, Herb."

In the months after he died, his friends from Arabica sent me drawings they had made of him, photographs, even a tape recording of one of his political rants. In the comic strip drawn by R. Crumb, Sid's name was unchanged, the beatnik beard a little less gray than it became, but still looking as if it had been trimmed with toenail scissors. Crumb, working as an artist for American Greetings in Cleveland, had been part of the radical bohemia in the Paris of Northeastern Ohio until he moved first to San Francisco and then to the south of France. An outpost of Arabica philosophers kept the faith in the North Coast, the Great Lake Erie country.

I carried his ashes back to San Francisco. I shipped his manuscript in four large boxes, which stand in a corner of my bedroom. Sometimes I carry one of the boxes into the sunny front room and excavate one geological layer or another. Stuck among the haphazard piles of paper, file folders, and notebooks are old letters from me, some dating back to my Army days during the War. I reread my letters, remembering myself as an eighteen-year-old stranger; I read a geological layer of the novel. The story abruptly shifts from Appalachia to Pittsburgh to Columbus. The plan is not revealed; the people, sometimes vividly evoked, just disappear and give way to new characters.

There are also journals in which he records his daydreams, his disputes with our mother and father, his ambitions. He writes about not sleeping, about sleeping too much, about passing time and not knowing how it has passed. As a freshman at Ohio State University, he describes riding a motorcycle — whose? — into the farm country outside Columbus instead of going to classes. He makes resolutions. He complains about not being able to keep his resolutions. He discusses Dostoyevsky, Kafka, and Faulkner with himself. He promises to get organized. "Weather permitting," he writes, with an echo of our father's lugubrious humor.

The manuscript ("The Novel") was stealing his life, his dreams taking over his world; at the same time, The Novel gave him a life, his hope that somehow, someday, he would carve out of this accumulating mass of paper his being in the world. As time went by, it diminished him, the rivulets of fantasy draining down the slope of years. The young man became an old man and remained a boy. He was afflicted with an impatient lyricism that never stopped to say: this much and no more; here's the beginning and here comes the need for an end; and now, wait, there *is* a way to stop.

After a while, I load the paper back into its box and think to myself: I've got to go at this systematically, try to figure out where something begins and where it ends. When he writes about the weather in Cleveland, I remember our hikes through the snow and our destination to hot chocolate at Clark's on Detroit Avenue; the snow is always new-fallen and white when I remember it. He was the guardian of childhood, the only person who still remembered our lives together in family. Now no one keeps me company in these memories, though his presence keeps flooding back in avalanches of geological layers, a lava flow of discovery, eagerness, hope, pain. I excavate in the California sun and find only more headlines from the *Plain Dealer*, more geological layers.

Sometimes I talk about him. I tell my children, his nieces and nephews, that he wasn't unhappy, and they tilt their heads and try to figure out why their dad is telling them something they know not to be the case. Okay, so he was unhappy, yes, but within the depression, kids . . . Let's see how I can explain this. Within the gloom and stasis . . . no. Within the unhappiness, he took pleasure in the newspaper, gossiping, coffee, his daydreams, his moments of resolute note taking and the clattering bursts of his garage-sale manual typewriter. Bits of envelopes, torn edges of newsprint stuck out of his pockets. Restlessly he gathered and sorted the materials for his geological layers. He never gave up. I love him "like a brother" — what an ambiguous expression that is.

His nephew, my son Ethan, strapped a guitar to his back when we hiked again into the Marin headlands to scatter Sid's ashes on the earth, in a stream, on a hillside. I carried the metal container from the mortuary in Cleveland and each of us reached into it for a handful. I remembered a Bob Dylan song for another loved one, asking for what cannot be given, "One more cup of coffee 'fore I go/To the valley below."

My daydream was interrupted by Ethan. He unsheathed his guitar and sang the song he had written, with the refrain, "It's okay, Sid. Sid, it's okay."

I keep a photograph in a place where I pass seldom so that familiarity won't make it invisible. It's from a time before he grew his beard; he is grinning, holding a pipe, poking the air with the pipe, telling a story. He's in command of an audience. The face I see when I remember him is the more recent one, perturbed and gray, his eyes squinting behind heavy glasses, not in command. The autopsy showed many problems — emphysema, arteries clogged, heart swollen, a malignancy. A doctor who interpreted the autopsy report for me said he would probably have died of the brain tumor and, hesitating, added, "You could think of a one-time heart attack as a blessing, if you like."

But that isn't what I think. I think of my telling him about a book and his saying, "Right, right, I'll get it at the library tomorrow." I think tomorrow he'll go to Arabica, hold his cup of black coffee (black coffee makes people crazy, our mother insisted), tell stories to his friends, tell a story he has just told once again, shout afterthoughts to the stories, vent opinions, and not know he was dying. He was just gonna get the book I recommended. He was just gonna call or write to me about it. He was just gonna see his travel agent about a ticket for a visit to San Francisco.

In recent years his face was deeply furrowed and I noted wrinkled grooves in his earlobes. I asked my doctor friend: "Was that a sign of heart — I read somewhere — circulation? Arteries?"

He answered: "I bet you have a subscription to *Prevention* with all those postcards so you can order herbal remedies. Keep up the ginkgo biloba, pal, especially if it makes you happy."

Not that my friend wasn't sympathetic; it's just that he was tired of perpetual seekers.

Sid was presented with gifts of sympathy, humor, understanding, and concern, but what he needed to understand, narrate, laugh about, and care for was too much for him to manage. He emitted opinions, often stubbornly wrong, distracted by his melancholy. He had lost pride. He had found grief early. His life was a long retreat. His sadness grew more intense as time went by. I want to think he never lost hope, although alone one morning, choking on his blood, struggling to sit up, he must have understood that his fifty-year-long unfinished novel was finally done with. The weather didn't permit.

In my bedroom sit these four crates of my brother's life, the uncharted universe of his dreaming. I carry the boxes into a sunnier room and try to read some of the mass of manuscript and then put the papers in their boxes and carry them back into the dark where he still lives in his geological layers.

8

Ghosts

Some marriages are best forgotten but unforgettable. An early first marriage gave me two children; that sums up the good part of it unless I include inoculation against certain future errors. (Not to be mean about it . . . but when I meet someone who looks, sounds, moves, or in some mysterious way reminds me of that first wife, there is only a blur in the universe as I run like the greatest track champion at the Marital Olympics staged on lovely Mount Agonistes.) I no longer need rage or nightmare starring the mother of the two daughters. Peace be on her soul.

My second wife, the one I loved, gave me three children, gave them to us together. We divorced and then, in an accident, she died. With an effort, I can bring some of our bad times forward in memory, like a recollected movie, but the vivid and lasting part of that marriage is the good and loving times. Her memory is still a treasure.

Then I was a bachelor again, *célibataire*, as the French put it in a word that seems overly finicky to an American ear. It doesn't mean celibate.

Divorced and grieving, a gray-flecked swinging single, I went out to sow my tame oats. At a party, the last time I saw "the love of my life"— that banal phrase is still alive — she smiled and winked approvingly across the room because she saw me with a pretty person. The man she planned to marry ambled up, grinning, abashed: "Herb, you raised a good wife."

I shrugged in lieu of saying thank you. He shrugged, meaning nothing but friendliness, hoping I wouldn't think he was being sarcastic. We were both holding glasses. I left him to chat with the pretty person while I went to make a birthday lunch date with my former wife. We settled on one of the quiet neighborhood cafés, which serve organic foods for San Franciscans planning to live forever. Her birthday gift was nicely wrapped at my door, waiting to be delivered, not that it would be forgotten. But I never gave it to her because she and the man she was planning to marry both died in a helicopter crash a few days later. I spent a morning telephoning our children away at colleges, one by one —"It's Dad, please sit down"— and then called her mother and father, and then my other children, listening to the cries, the choking, the screams.

It's been said that a person always remembers the last time he saw a beloved. That doesn't cover the matter here. Each time I saw her seemed like the first time.

At the funeral service after Melissa was killed, our son Ethan had arranged a playing of the Bob Dylan song which asks for "one more cup of coffee before I go." I can't hear that song without the terrible ache of loss, unrecoverable losses, here in the other valley below.

Every grief is unique. Life doesn't necessarily make us better; that's not life's business. Life gives what it gives, takes back what it takes back, and it's our business to sort things out for ourselves as best we can.

★ ★ ★

I tell my stories to my children, my daguerreotype memories of their grandparents, legends of the parents of grandparents, portraits all time-rubbed at the edges: Cleveland, once an industrial metropolis proud of its skilled labor and its ethnic enclaves, its daily newspapers in Hungarian and Polish; the Army during *my* war, trying to pass on memories of the friends now disappeared . . . I try to plant my own Jewish history in my half-Jewish children because no history should disappear. The ancestors I never knew are still a part of our lives.

In the telling of my stories, these lives take shapes that are no doubt distorted on behalf of significance, laughter, or a clarity untrue to history. (There may not really have been a textbook for Polish immigrants to Cleveland with the title *Polish Up Your English.* I probably had dinner with my parents in at least one restaurant without a gypsy violinist.)

Ari accuses me of saying he asked at age twelve what the world was like before herpes and AIDS. ("There were giants in those days, my son.") My daughters are amazed that I transported myself through America by thumb and even hitchhiked in France with my first wife. Ethan listens patiently as I repeat the tale of my near court-martial for dropping my rifle and swinging on a fellow soldier during basic training. (He stepped on my heels, muttering, "Jew, Jew, Jew," as we marched in morning formation across the red sands of Fort Bragg, North Carolina.)

The captain gave me a choice of a court-martial or a public boxing match in the Company day room. An improvised ring was set up with ropes tied to chairs. We strapped on 16-ounce gloves and flailed at each other until we could no longer move. I resmell after all these years the stink of my own sweat and that of my adversary. It was all part of the war against Nazism, now as real and as unreal as Brownie cameras and the appetite for frozen Milky Way candy bars.

So what was the world like before herpes and AIDS? And you hitchhiked in France with Edith, whom they met in her later life, when she was a five-star traveler, not a hair out of place, fanatic about her expensive pumps? We can't step in the same river twice, but we can recall snapshots of the long-departed flow and different footwear.

Along with the shared implications of their complicated family stand the unsharable moments remembered only by their father — firelight on the half-turned face of their mother, the sounds of Bob Dylan songs before these children were conceived, how a father's arm was warmed when their mother put her hand on it, how his chest felt when she laid her arm over it as lovers subsided into sleep. Such matters between lovers should not be lost.

And then, at the end of love, also fixed in memory, comes the vision of a woman strolling naked out of the bathroom and saying, "Okay, you want me, take me now so I can get a decent night's rest." She took my arm like a happy lover and then she didn't.

Often the no longer married man's bed is empty when he wishes it weren't. Sometimes there's a sag in the spirit, a gloom in the afternoon, an emptiness in the day, a three A.M. awakening to futile thoughts of futility. The legs start from sleep as if to run from life and the eyes stare into the dark. Life has gone on so long, but why, to what end or good?

The problem might be low blood pressure, a glucose dip. But that's not the problem. Even loved children can't be expected to touch the body and soul with all that body and soul crave. Once a well-wisher, a close friend, suggested a solution to this late-life loneliness. "Give up about love, what we used to think was love. Find a companion, that's enough."

The blood rushed to my head. I was infuriated. "That would be death. Living with someone because it's a warm body, someone to sit in front of the television with — no, thanks. No!"

We finished our meal in separate realms of silence. An exchange of services may be enough for some. There are those men and women who live with companions in marital irritation, which is worse than loneliness; or dwell with the warm body out of habit and a sense of duty; or endure in grief and conflict because they see no exit. I know a longtime couple who bicker over which one of them is more loved by their dog. ("She's getting fat! You spoil her! No wonder she jumps into your lap! You give her cookies when I'm not looking!" "They're called biscuits. You sneak them to her, too.")

I'll take insomnia over boredom or desolation. If alone and needing to be driven to the emergency room, I'll call a cab or 911. Or if I cannot, I won't.

Stubbornly, I'm still ready to fall in love again tomorrow morning at dawn as I walk down Russian Hill to breakfast. The bathroom mirror informs me that I am no longer twenty-seven years old and the girl of my dreams is either still asleep or staring at the ceiling, wondering which unknown man's magic will suddenly wake her from her own dreams.

It seems that I extend my life backward in memory, forward in expectation. Yet I'm aware of the facts. Arise, dawn dreamer, come out to the café for coffee and the lover waiting there for you.

Dying, Does It Mean Anything? Does It Just Happen? Why Not Just Relax and Enjoy It?

My first childhood friend to die a natural death, not an unnatural war death, was a scientist with a brilliant career and a better one to come if he lived past the age of forty. He didn't. It's odd to describe Hodgkin's disease as natural, but so it is, like all diseases, part of our error-prone organic systems.

When I visited him late in this procedure of dying, propped up against pillows in bed, he remarked with a smile, "You know, another few years and they'll have a remedy, probably a cure."

I didn't say "So hang on," because I knew he couldn't anymore, not any longer. I told my young daughters what was happening, I wanted them to say good-bye. Judy, soon returning to her mother's custody, stared. He was so thin and wasted that he hardly dented the pillows. She said, "I'm going to write to you."

He grinned. He understood what she meant: You're a polite person, so you have to answer my letters. I'll keep you alive by keeping you obliged, because you've known me all your life and you must keep writing to me . . . She knew the rules for courtesy.

Then, while my daughters were having milk and cookies with his wife, out of their hearing, he said good-bye to me, but then asked, "What do you do when you know the end is near?"

I didn't know. What came out of my face was: "Hey, just relax and enjoy it."

He laughed. I laughed. The end came a few days later.

I still don't know what to do if the end is near. Pretending it's not is an illogical option. Postponing it if possible is a temporary option. Now, more than forty years later, the best I can think of doing is still just to enjoy it.

I've learned to watch myself fall asleep. The smoky wisps of memory condense into images; stories from the past are played in revival; I'm not distracted by a daytime soundtrack of tinnitis. I float, sometimes with pleasure, sometimes anxiously, into new narratives, accumulating from elements of the old ones. And then I'm gone, the dream happening without me.

When the wisps form into nightmare, my leg jerks, I jump awake. *Who! What! Where am I!* Those are not questions; they are cries into the dark. When the story of my past or future is full of dread, I get up and walk in the nocturnal streets of whatever town I'm in, San Francisco, New York, Cleveland, Paris, Port-au-Prince. In Dakar, I was arrested as a spy, saboteur, or bank robber, probably all three, merely for standing outside a bank to admire its architecture, which combined international glass and cement with elaborate twists and knobs modeled on the patriotic Senegalese tree, the baobab. The police wanted to know why I performed this act of standing in the middle of the night. My explanation, that it was the Christmas season and my former wife and children were elsewhere and I was jet-lagged, struck them as illogical. I rethought the matter. I then emitted a eulogy of the delightful hospitality of the Senegalese people, concluding with the awe I felt before the stirring, glorious, nut-bearing baobab. I spoke French more rapidly than is my wont; I don't speak Wolof. Eloquence, plus a small *pourboire*, softened their hearts, and I returned to my hotel to sleep the sleep of the justly absolved.

In the world of night, trees stand like sentinels to guard our unrest, even trees made of glass and molded concrete.

Once I watched male and female *coco de mer* palm trees bending to each other in the tropical breezes near a beach at the Indian Ocean in the Seychelles. Legend tells that they mate like teenagers when others sleep, but there could be no lovemaking for the *coco de mer* during that night — I was spying on them. In Port-au-Prince, the city groans, awake and throbbing in the dark, charcoal cooking fires burning, ghostly peasant women, Mesdames Saras, barefoot, silently striding down to the markets with baskets balanced on their heads. The streets are stony, hilly, distressed, and ominous at that hour; I don't go far.

If the insomnia is that of jet lag or regret, I do my best to turn the corner into pleasure, studying the enjoyment of melancholy, spying on the other night people, listening under windows, relishing the wildness that grows in the interstices of every city. At night, weeds and junk vegetation are usually gray, but sometimes, if headlights approach, nature's stubborn persistence flashes as green as under sunshine. Then the vehicle passes.

In dreams, I still jump over roofs to escape pursuers. I can fly and they can't. I still meet the beautiful and complicated woman I married and thought I knew, or the brooding one bent over a notebook in the diner on West Twenty-third Street in Manhattan, whom I never spoke to or saw again. I see my dead brother, my dead parents, my dead wife, and am comforted by their presence even if only when I'm asleep.

When I'm asleep, I'm still awake. The inevitable erotic dreams remind me that life goes on. I'm happy that nightmares still frighten, as they used to when I cried out and my mother came running to the room. And then I turned them into stories, which I told my thrilled brother in his twin bed against the opposite wall.

In nightmares, relentless devils chase me; they can run faster, but they can't leap over roofs as I can, so when I see a roof, I run toward it and gain space between me and dire fate. I'm pretty clever that way. In erotic dreams, gracious women beckon, sometimes the wife I loved, sometimes the woman in the all-night diner on West Twenty-third Street, sometimes no one I can remember but will surely find again in another dream.

Tinnitis is high and shrill, a whine, inappropriate, like the sound of fluorescent tubes in a rustbelt factory. No one else hears that buzz, that whine, it's all mine, its up to me to fix it. What can I do? Get anxious, call the audiologist, try white noise machines, try hearing non-aids, or get used to it?

I decided: okay, get used to it.

Now, I'm used to it. There should be fat flies buzzing around my head, attracted by the humid smell of old dreams. I understand just how they would feel — hungry, leaping, colliding in air, eager to suck juice and copulate. Dr. Shirley Li, the nice audiologist, does her best, but only for my hearing.

It's about as long now since the end of World War II, "my" war, as the span of time from the end of the Spanish-American War to the summer of 1956 when I happened upon an eerie gathering of ancients in Saratoga Springs, New York, at what might have been the last convention of its veterans. The leafy street was crowded with a shocking collection of the lame, the blind, the withered, the wheelchaired, the blinking and lost. I thought I had entered a madness, I thought this vision of the future was some sort of unholy punishment. An August wind barely stirred the branches overhead. A pennant hung loose: REMEMBER THE MAINE.

This vivid booty from the past stations me in the present time of my life. I still can taste the cold draft beer I drank in a sidestreet trucker's tavern, asking myself if I would ever be one of the veterans I had just seen, lolling in a wheelchair pushed by a woman in a white nylon uniform.

Old is not a process; it's a state of being. The process I'm in is *aging*, a different matter. I'm heading someplace not yet defined, growing not old but into further aging. When aging stops, then I'll be old. I'll do my best for it not to stop until my oldness is merely synonymous with death. When a French or Haitian friend greets me with the traditional *"Mon vieux!"* I grin, and he grins because this familiar "My old!" means "my friend-who-is-still-and-always-in-my-heart." (The French aren't generally given to explicit open expressions of sentiment. *"Mon vieux"* is often administered with a mitigating irony, shoulders and mouth twitching.)

A longtime pal, a fellow striver whose work I admired, a man with whom I had shared many meals, whose wife I liked, whose divorce gave me sorrow, moved to Arizona for reasons that seemed good to him (sun, air, peace and quiet in which to breathe the air, bask in the sunlight, calm his striving spirit). We visited each other, exchanged letters, spoke on the phone.

One day I received a short note from him, stating curtly, "Please do not contact me again until one year from the above date."

I immediately wrote to him: "Have I offended you in some way?" He wrote back with one word: "No." I persisted: "Then what's going on?"

He replied with a few more words. "You may communicate with me again on the date previously indicated."

And that was the last I heard from him. If there was anger, I never discovered its cause. He died before "the date previously indicated." What grief, what deterioration, what stubborn shutting of doors?

Another friend treated his agonizing stomach cancer as a comic occasion. When he decided to put himself out of his pain, making sure he had enough pills and vodka, he said good-bye to his wife as usual when she went off to her job, then retreated to their backyard so that he would not make a mess in the house. He left a note by his body in the garden. "Warning: Anyone who resuscitates me, I will sue. If you're just a poor shlub, I'll take you to Small Claims Court."

The novelist Mordecai Richler, dealing with kidney cancer, commented in his familiar comic style: "When my children visit, I don't see offspring, I see potential organ donors."

The journalist Paul Jacobs, in the grip of lung cancer, which he believed he contracted from breathing the particles during his investigation of uranium tailings in Nevada, visited dying soldiers who had worked on atomic testing for the Army. Before he died, he finished a documentary film on the subject. He was delighted when a terminal patient croaked at him from his bed: "Mr. Jacobs, what are you doing here? You look worse than I do."

Paul thought that made great footage. He was happy in his perishing to be able to argue his points. I still keep his photograph in my study and think: Way to go, Paul.

In the late life memoirs of Charles de Gaulle, he writes that old age is a shipwreck. De Gaulle felt defeated and abandoned. But his old age was more like a leaky sailboat thrashing in the storm before it finally went down.

Loss needs to be acknowledged. Growing old is something I have suspicions about. It's a by-product of other losses. Death is something I can only dimly imagine, fear, expect. I admire its absoluteness. I don't know anyone out there, perhaps one with a white beard and kind eyes, who can provide me with further explanations. I have to make my own way with piecemeal notions about the mysterious destination.

Last words are supposed to be especially important as a clue to the meaning of it all. Henry James said something like "Now, at last, the distinguished thing"— sticking to the end with his Jamesian style of elegant moroseness. Beethoven is supposed to have said "More light! More light!" That's better, not so pretentious, and full of Beethovenesque imperative. William Saroyan commented that he knew all men are mortal, but didn't think it applied to him. "Now what?" he asked. That was proper and fine. But I most admire the last words of Alfred Jarry, author of *King Ubu*, who noticed his admirers gathered around him, hoping for a final revelation, although he could barely utter a sound. When someone bent an ear to his lips to catch his dying revelation, Jarry whispered: "Anybody got a toothpick?"

If I had Jarry's photo, I'd place it next to Paul Jacobs's. Death is the end, not like sleep. Sleep is crowded with dreams, activity. The analogy of sleep with death offers comfort I don't want. The comfort I have now is that the past will live because of what I've done, the children I have, their children, and the time I put my wife's initials in wet sidewalk cement. Just because I'm no longer walking, you won't dig up my heartfelt sidewalk inscription, will you?

My Own Father, Who Are Not in Heaven

Pascal's Wager can be interpreted as suggesting that there would be nothing lost if one believes in God and He doesn't exist, but a lot lost if God happens to exist and one doesn't believe. Pascal was French, ironic and uneasy. He wanted to maximize his chances for a cozy afterlife in a place something like the Tuileries gardens in Paris. On a good day.

William James took the Wager in a more American direction. God may not exist, heaven may not exist, the chances are they don't. But what does it hurt to believe? Folks seem to need belief, and not just folks but also William James. Faith makes a person feel better. Boston is cold; the winter is black in Cambridge. The evidence for belief as comfort is persuasive. And if God really presides up above, a person would be in better shape after death, with a chance to enjoy eternity. Reach for stars; why not?

William James's *The Varieties of Religious Experience* is a long sigh of relief. He was subject to depressions. Now he felt better.

My father had his own response to Blaise Pascal and William James. He died in Cleveland in his nineties, but he was once a boy in Kamenetz-Podolsk, escaping to America because he didn't want any timeless village life and also didn't want to be drafted into the Czar's army. At age thirteen, he lit out for the territory ahead, westward across the mountain-high waves of the Atlantic to where he could determine the truth of the one sentence he had learned in English: "There's gold in the streets of New York." I used to tell him that if he had only taken the name Streets instead of Gold, I would be tall, blue-eyed, and blond.

What he was looking for, and what he found, was freedom from doctrine, freedom to define his life for himself. American freedom was his spiritual need.

On one of my last visits to Cleveland during his ninety-fourth year, he greeted me by thrusting a letter into my hands. It was addressed to him from my cousin, the Reverend Herman Rothblatt, who had been born again, that is, Born Again, while in art school. (Perhaps, as a Jewish lad, this was something like being born for the first time after an erroneous twenty years in this vale of tears and overconsumption of sugary treats.) The letter said, "Dear Uncle Sam: Now that you are about to die, isn't it time for you to accept Jesus as your personal Savior?"

"What's this? What's this? What's this crap?" my father asked.

I didn't need to discuss Pascal or William James with Dad. Without knowing anything about French Jansenism or American Pragmatism, he had already come to his own answer, which I might call Sam Gold's Wager.

In later years, the Reverend Herman Rothblatt discovered a cure for cancer, but after I neglected to invest in his Hong Kong–based startup company, we seem to have lost track of each other.

My father made a certain impression on his world. He then diminished and died. But lives on in memory.

9

Edward J. Pols

My only friend remaining from the wartime U.S. Army, the last one I kept in continuous contact with, has died. Ed Pols, Edward J. Pols, taught philosophy at Bowdoin College, but when I first met him we were both in a military intelligence program, he learning German, I learning Russian. He was already married to thoughtful and gentle Eileen, proud of his good Catholic rearing, and like me a consumer of the cookies left on trays in Army mess halls. When we were both punished for non-cookie-related offenses with 48-hour weekend K.P. instead of being allowed off the base, I tried to look on the bright side of having my hands eaten by strong soap while I scratched at pots with G.I. Brillo-like Brillo. "Well, at least this is an experience. We can learn from it."

I was thinking it would deepen my soul, sharpen my prose, make more poignant my verse.

He answered: "An hour of this experience would suffice." He had already studied the pre-Socratic philosophers. I was eighteen, he was a few years older. All the Brillo adventure deepened, soulwise, was my compassion for myself.

In due course, the fighting stopped in Europe and Ed

was the officer in charge of a detachment based in Berlin, traveling through the occupied lands, tracking down art treasures looted by the Nazis. Because his team had to deal with Soviet forces, they needed a Russian interpreter. He sent me word: Would I like to be part of the art recovery effort?

Would I! I was burning to see some sort of useful action before shipping out to make contact with the Soviet armies scheduled to drive into China against the Japanese when the Americans landed from the Pacific. In addition to learning Russian, I spoke a bit of French. I also hoped to unearth French treasures, such as any delicate Fifis in wooden clogs who might come dawdling in my path. I knew a song, *"Viens, viens, dans mes bras / Je te donne du chocolat."*

My orders were on the way. One morning the captain in charge of our little group of Russian interpreter-translators strolled over to stand nearby and observe my activity. His arms were crossed in his usual expression of exasperation. He was in his impeccable tailored uniform with the dashing red cavalry scarf dashingly draped over his dashing shoulders. I knew Ed's request had descended through channels to him. After a while, he crooked a finger at me. *Come here, soldier.* I approached and saluted.

The U.S. Army in its occasional wisdom during a great war tried to filter out incompetent officers, sending them where they could do less harm. Captain Collins was of this select group, shifted away from possible severe damage to run a group of military intelligence trainees, making sure we buttoned and dressed according to the rules, kept our shoes shined and bedding tight, didn't roll up our khaki sleeves on or off duty, and expressed proper respect for marginal-I.Q. commissioned officers.

"Gold," he said icily, "I suppose you know a request has come from the German field of operations . . ." He paused.

"Yes, sir."

". . . a request to assign you to a special detachment in Berlin."

"Yes, sir."

He glared until I lowered my eyes. "And I'm sure this is an assignment you would enjoy . . ."

I had the good sense, or maybe the bad sense, to say nothing. A flicker of pleasure crossed the face of Captain Collins, not a smile but a dashing cavalry version of a happy grimace, a twitch of one corner of a stern, stalwart, low-I.Q. commissioned ROTC mouth. He was enjoying himself as my own nineteen-year-old self sweated, sleeves correctly rolled down and buttoned. Once he had caught me out without correct sleeves and threatened me with a court-martial, although I wasn't sure this was a capital offense. ". . . enjoy more, rather preferably, than serving as previously designated the uniform you somewhat sloppily wear."

I decided not to say "Yes, sir."

"However," he said, "I have declared you essential where you are, Private."

Where I was at that moment was off to the side of an improvised volleyball court on a level grassy stretch of the Cornell University campus. We had been sent there to refresh and improve our grasp of Russian. My Russian was already well refreshed, well improved. That morning our little group

of Military Intelligence trainees was playing essential volleyball in Russian. I was not allowed to go to Berlin.

A few years after the war, as a young professor at Bowdoin,
Ed Pols suggested me as a candidate for an English instructor-
ship. The college invited me to Brunswick, Maine. On the
one hand, I needed a job (wife, one baby, another on the
way); on the other hand, I wasn't sure I wanted to move to
Maine; but on the third hand — in this matter, as in others,
exceptions must be made to the rule that folks generally have
only two hands — my dear friends Ed and Eileen were there.
Unfortunately, the resident poet, a Maine institution, argued
that they already had enough New York Jews on faculty. If he
had pointed this out to me personally, I might have informed
him that I was a Cleveland, actually Lakewood, Ohio, Jew.

In the darkness of age, I hope not to rage against the dying of the light; rather, to find a lantern. But will it run out
of batteries? At this stage, I see the past not as mere nostalgia
but as part of the present. Therefore: my new wife and I are
in Boston; Ed and Eileen drive down from Maine to visit
with us . . . It was the time of the flower explosion in San
Francisco and America; the Age of Aquarius was the permanent year. Tourists, we four chose to celebrate our meeting
with an elegant lunch at the Ritz-Carlton hotel.

It was not the Age of Aquarius at the Ritz-Carlton
maître d's desk. Professor Pols, his wife, and the newlywed
Golds were turned away. My hair was rather long, but that
was not the problem. Melissa was wearing a miniskirt. Her
long legs were the problem.

Later, Eileen wrote an epic poem to celebrate the joy of being denied shrimp Creole at the Ritz-Carlton in Boston because of the skirt of my bride, a recent Radcliffe graduate whose mother's maiden name, Cushing, was that of a well-known family in Boston. "As flies to wanton boys are we to the gods," was how I explained the maître d's expulsion of us from lunch. I borrowed the comment from King Lear.

My lantern finds corners of pleasure that relieve loneliness in the long passage through time when Melissa, Eileen, and Ed are all absent.

Perhaps as karmic redressment for the failure to employ me as a Russian interpreter in postwar Europe, plus the failure even to achieve shrimp Creole at the Ritz, I was invited to participate in a conference on "The Foundations of Cultural Unity" at Bowdoin College. Gathered there were Nobel Prize scientists, a Texas philosopher-bureaucrat, a Harvard psychologist, a painter, a novelist, a poet. For the word "conference," I would prefer the more accurate term, "foundation-supported boondoggle." On an early morning hike into town, Henry Murray, the Harvard psychologist, aged close to ninety, offered me an apology for his continuing vivacity. "I stand on my head every morning. And I think. It keeps the blood from coagulating, and then the things that come up push ideas and blood through my arteries."

"It seems to work," I said.

"And the veins. You think there's a muffin store open this early? I don't diet." He took a deep breath. "I enjoy this Maine air either way, on my feet or upside down."

It was working. The boondoggle provided me with a valuable foundation-supported stroll with Henry Murray.

I continued to keep contact with Ed and Eileen Pols as they aged, she gradually slipping from her sly amusement at the ways of the world into Alzheimer's and silence, Ed continuing his youthful enthusiasm for philosophy, the traditional verse he wrote, his college. When he developed cancer, he still sounded like the intense and boyish basketball player I remembered. When he was supposed to die, he didn't. But then, finally, around the time he sent me a new sheaf of poems about "our" war, he did die.

My last friend from those three years in the U.S. Army. From now on, I have to do my own remembering.

As long as my friends from the War are young, I can be young. As long as my friends from the postwar bohemian migration to Paris are young, I'm young. But they're not anymore, except for those who found the way to be forever young by dying early. Still, growing old seems only a threat, a rumor.

I first met Ned Rorem, composer and diarist, during that pre-Beatnik crusade of ambitious would-bees who boarded the ships bound for France and Paris, "capital of hope and paradise of misery." He was a handsome, smiling person, marked for stardom, a charmer, an escort for le Tout Paris and le Tout Demimonde, smooth of skin, sparkling of smile, boyish of profile. Everyone but a few sullen killjoys expected him to become a world-famous composer, everyone was sure of it, except for those mealy jealous rivals who muttered that he would end up merely well-known.

My ritual, when we meet over the years since, is to say, "You're still a promising young lad, Ned, so maybe I can be, too." We were born the same year.

When we happened to meet at an arts festival at Ball State University in Indiana, his home state, he told me that the local museum had acquired portraits of early American presidents and the local newspaper headlined the news: WASHINGTON AND JEFFERSON HUNG BY BALLS.

In recent years there have been tribute recitals of Ned Rorem's art songs, described as valedictory events. I need to see him again to ask: Aren't you still the boy genius of the art song profession? Aren't we still hanging out among the Gauloise Bleu and Gitane smokers at Saint-Germain-des-Prés? And what about those aquiline social ladies from the Faubourg Saint-Honoré who present their hawk noses in profile as soon as a Leica appears? If we only misbehave within the strict limits prescribed for artistic young Americans, these ladies or one of the cologned gentlemen may invite us for a weekend in the ancestral country château which the German occupants were too courteous to damage. (*Ned from Indiana, this is Herb from Cleveland calling.*)

Unlike Mason Hoffenberg, eventual coauthor with Terry Southern of the novel *Candy*, my colleague in the more Left Bank implantation of would-bees, Ned Rorem practiced survival by upper-Bohemian Paris propriety. Mason preferred to practice New York con, selling hashish to existentialists thrilled by having an American dealer. He got extra francs and extra credit for his product. I accompanied him to the Hôtel de Seine where a famous philosopher bought a stash at an inflated price. Mason winked at me (*Pay attention!*) during this successful mission. "Fucking snob thinks it's genuine marijuana imported from Harlem," he told me over cheese and a baguette at the nearby café La Palette. Mason's treat.

The expectation of eternal youth, like the expectation of eternal life, is a plan to slide up a slippery slope. Up doesn't normally occur in nature's flow. Immortality only lasts for a little while in the world of human fact; yet imagination, even ones of lyrical pessimism, struggles with the concept of non-being. The evidence of disappearance might seem to brook no argument. The notion of heaven suits some, answering their needs, supplying a future without argument, although sometimes depending on good behavior. Hell and the recently defunct doctrine of limbo are efforts to deal with the subject.

Heaven, hell, and the equivocation of limbo are of no help to me. I should fear becoming a sort of earth slug, deeply buried among the death of others, living off their remains and also off my own past. There's a limitless supply of past; the future diminishes. Of course, heaven would be a fine solution if it existed. In my dreams, I merely persevere. I fly over roofs, sometimes escaping pursuers, sometimes playing like a bird. When I wake, I try to decide if it was a nightmare or a thrilling and extravagant freedom.

I don't always know.

In the world of dailiness, there's a gloomy contradiction between the assumption of life variously persevering and the notice, which doesn't escape me, that others keep disappearing. If I followed that chipper command, "Live every day as if it's your last," I'd spend the day in bitter complaint. Instead, what most of us do is live as if the living will continue until we hear the rattle in our throats. We don't detect it just now when we head for a breakfast of lightly scrambled eggs or we meet the direct gaze of a loved child or merely watch the urban hummingbirds busy in the tree outside our window.

Friends pass into mystery. I stare at their tracks in my address book. I can't bear to cross out the names, I leave them, I still remember telephone numbers. On a Sunday afternoon I go to the phone and start to press the keys for Sid, my beloved baby brother. No, that number in Cleveland doesn't answer. I stop. I think of Ed and Eileen Pols in Maine. I think, *Ed, Eileen*, and then I rummage in my head for someone I can still reach.

Grief is no fun; absence is not the best space to live in. Forgetting would be worse. Losses accumulate, a debt that someday, no matter what I do to postpone it, I'll have to pay with myself.

10

Advanced Sub-Acute Thinking

Craig Nebisher, an advanced-thinking prof with an even more advanced-thinking wife, which was how things sometimes went during the first swift blooming of the Women's Movement, took an initiative by joining his daughters for their Afro-Cuban dance lessons. It was what the absent mother would have done, had she not been absent. Other fathers merely watched on folding chairs, occasionally clattering to the floor if they dozed and slumped. Craig showed them up as the uptight, drag-ass parents they were. He wiggled to the beat of Afro-Cuban recordings. "Daddy! Please!" his daughters cried. "Daddy, you weigh a ton! Stop!"

He compromised with his delightful progeny. He didn't stop, but resolved to lose weight, really do it this time, and in fact he believed the circumference of his haunches was diminishing. Caring for two daughters, cleaning house, making meals, helping with homework, washing tights in lukewarm water, using loving hands and soap and then letting the tights dry on towels, seemed to work haunch wonders he had previously been unable to work. He no longer looked so much like a beached whale, flopping to Afro-Cuban rhythms. He no longer packed tonnage, shaming his daughters. "My thunder thighs," he told me, "I measure them with a tape measure . . ."

He left the sentence unfinished. Or maybe it was finished, but I expected more. He didn't want to boast in that obsolete macho way. He lowered his eyes. He widened his horizons downward. The Third World had so much to teach about rhythm, closeness to the soil, a quiverload of indigenous stuff, not to mention his personal discovery that Third World dances could do wonders for overgrown thighs. He demonstrated by pinching himself. "We were programmed to be hunter-gatherers," he explained, "but the future is in nurturing."

"In a better world," I said.

"Hopefully."

"One spouse at a time," I both thought and said. He took no offense, such being the primitive habit of macho hunters and many gatherers, too.

Busy taking no offense, Craig remained silent for a moment. He eyed the rainbow epaulets that had been sewed onto my shirt by my wife. She liked to exercise her gift for irony. Although epaulets suggested military officers, epaulets made of rainbow ribbons suggested multicultural allegiances. The point, being unclear, could await further developments. Further developments followed.

Craig suggested humbly that it might be a good idea to be more like him, evolved — he had in mind greater issues than thighs. He credited his spouse, recently renamed for Diana the Huntress, with evolving him. Like Ted Natter, he couldn't have done it alone. Both Craig and Ted hesitated to criticize my spouse, whom I still called my "wife," but made it clear that the patriarchal hunter–gatherer paradigm was so over in a world that hungered for faithful caregiving.

My wife (spouse) grinned when I passed on the news. "Next time I see them, I'll wear my headband." She wrapped it around her forehead, suggesting Native American credentials, although she wasn't a Native American. It was a look we both liked, but without a feather, not warlike. We were consistent lovers of peace. She was one of the few young women in our local peacemaking crowd who opposed wearing cartridge belts as a fashion statement during picketing missions at the Federal Building in San Francisco. Cartridge belts plus chants of "U.S. Out of Viet Nam!" sent a mixed message, whereas a lovely ribbon wrapped around the forehead sent the message: I'm together, I'm a together person, we can all keep our brains together, it's still possible, guys.

This was a time of great innovation in Lifestyle and disease discovery. Craig's wife, Diana, with a devoted husband and two sunny daughters, wondered if she had the right to contentment when so many east Asians were dying in east Asia and so many sisters were being pressured to have sex with men who didn't necessarily deserve them. Out of solidarity with the suffering masses and victims of marital disrespect, she decided to take leave of her husband and children for a six-month retreat at an all-womyn commune in Santa Cruz. At the family conference where she announced her move, she explained that she was not a lesbian, but an explorer of alternative lifestyles. That was the plan. While she explained, her younger daughter explored the cleansing, irrigating sensation of tears and Craig smilingly developed a frontal lobe headache.

"Stop your crying," said Mom to Liz. "I'll keep in touch."

She kept in touch with Monday postcards, plus get-well cards when the girls caught the flu. Unfortunately, to telephone would interrupt the flow of alternative lifestyle, but she sent spiritual love vibes shooting down California Route One, the scenic road from Santa Cruz to San Francisco. She was learning from her mates in the commune that often a man would say he respected a woman before they had sex, but would just turn his hairy back on her afterward, snoring away without a care in the world, neglecting to nurture the recently discovered G-spot. On one of her postcards, she wrote to Liz that soon she might be told by a boy that he respected her, but she should watch out. Diana was learning to become a really together *her*man being. The patriarchy had conspired to hide the news of the G-spot for thousands of years. Women were not going to take it anymore.

Meanwhile, Craig was exploring the headache and depression lifestyle. He feared he hadn't even paid enough attention to the A- through F-spots. Through one of his colleagues at San Francisco State, he found a doctor to diagnose his condition. "Sub-acute epilepsy," Craig explained to me. "Check it out for yourself."

I hadn't heard of this disease.

"Epilepsy without any symptoms of epilepsy."

"Pardon?"

"Well, do you have headaches sometimes? bad dreams? Are you depressed sometimes?"

I checked through my history. "At times, all of the above."

Craig threw up his hands. "You see? It's a done deal. A

clear case of . . ." He lowered his voice. He was proud to share. "Epilepsy in the sub-acute form."

The treatment consisted of vitamins, deep breathing, and regular office visits to the sub-acute epilepsy specialist. Since I already was a frequent breather and vitamin buyer, my problems were only intermittent. But with regular office visits, I could eliminate the need for long walks and coffee, my usual remedies.

"Forget the blues and gather the roses," Craig advised, his voice no longer lowered, startling the folks at the next table.

"So how's your wife doing?"

He made a little wince. "She wants me to refer to her as spouse, not wife. My spouse is coming home in another forty-three days."

"You're counting," I said. Life gave him many occasions for sub-acute fits, such as friends like me. There were even complications for him in his daughters' (and his) dance classes. He launched a student rebellion, joined by no one, not even his daughters, against a choreographed series of leaps and bounds accompanying the recording of a non-Afro-Cuban song:

Mama, get the hammer,
There's a fly on baby's head

"This is no time for joking about child abuse," he told the instructor, Gwana Akumba, and stamped his bare foot. "I won't participate." He warmed his hurt heel in his hand; he forgot he hadn't been wearing shoes when he stamped. He glared from a folding chair while the other dancers, sellouts to the military-industrial-folkdancing complex, enacted life on a front porch without insect screens. Craig was a pioneer in suffering new diseases and principle-related conditions, such as sub-acute epilepsy and a foot hurt in the line of duty.

He explored the frontiers of manly feminism. This was a time of incest survival groups to rescue survivors, sometimes victims whose fathers, uncles, or brothers never actually did anything untoward, but may well have thought of it. In Mill Valley, a weekly Affluence Visualization Seminar gathered future millionaires who were not yet rich because they hadn't correctly visualized wealth (also hadn't accumulated a lot of money). A person couldn't venture out in the Bay Area without finding a remedy for a nefarious condition never before diagnosed. Cures struggled to keep pace with syndromes.

During one military crisis, my college classmate Allen Ginsberg — sometimes my friend, sometimes not, sometimes my friend again — asked the Hell's Angels to rescind their offer to serve as "gorillas" in Viet Nam. He didn't criticize Oakland chapter president Sonny Barger's spelling of "guerrillas" in his telegram to United States president Richard Nixon because Allen was a compassionate, nonjudgmental peace advocate. Instead, as a fallback position, Allen recruited what he called "a trained corps of disciplined fairies" to unbutton the jeans of the Hell's Angels and fellate them into love and understanding. History does not record President S. Barger's response to Allen's Zen-inspired project, but we do know that the war in Viet Nam eventually ended.

Satanic rituals were only a few years off — fourteen-year-olds impregnated so that the fetuses could be torn out and used in unspeakable ceremonies, generally in secluded woods. The FBI uncovered no evidence of this because the FBI was complicit. A twelve-hundred-page book connected the Mafia, the Kennedys, the Illuminati, and certain Elders with a plot to conceal the fact that Moses was actually an Egyptian. I only read a two-hundred-page summary of *The Gemstone Papers*, but the friend who offered it to me was the Jewish founder of a chain of no-preservative muffin shops, and as a Jewish person himself, assured me that no anti-Semitism was involved.

Waking up to the sounds of the Jefferson Airplane, Joan Baez, or a cover of that anthem about sitting by the dock of the bay was always an adventure. You could esteem both Sam Cooke and Bob Dylan; only fools liked Donovan. The woman teaching the lessons of *The Gemstone Papers* on FM radio in San Jose linked California politics, Alexander Hamilton, the Mafia, Pope John XXIII, Zionism, Quaker Oats, and the Kellogg's cereal monolith in a way that was difficult to follow unless you paid attention. But people were distracted by their own lives; another cunning trick of the Illuminati.

After Diana MacKenzie-Nebisher's brief investigatory foray into the herperson's commune in Santa Cruz, she returned to find that Craig had taken advantage of her absence to learn to bake cakes and what he called a "decadent" chocolate and cherry pie. Spouse turned up her adorable nose at the pie. Craig explained that "decadent" was how all the great chefs described rich chocolate desserts. Gourmet cheficizing was only one of the things he had studied during Spouse's marriage sabbatical. Yon Cassius had a sulky and larded look; he thought too much and renewed an old hobby, overeating. He had misplaced the tape measure with which he measured his thighs. Such men are dangerous, mostly to themselves.

"Well, bye-bye to that," snapped Spouse, meaning cherry and chocolate pie. She had learned different things in Santa Cruz, including how to spill pig's blood on the Miss America parade. Back with her family, she wrote long letters, not just Monday postcards, to her fellow communards. Solidarity Forever was the reason. She propped up her broadened horizons in order to preserve both vertical and horizontal dimension.

"Pig's blood?" her younger daughter asked. "On a car?"

"Was it a convertible?" her other daughter asked.

"With the top down," said the warrior, home from her wars. "On her stupid pink gown."

"Yucch, so gross, Mom," said one of the daughters.

"You can call me Diana," the mother said.

As the years sped by and the snows melted in those regions that include snow among the weather choices, and then the spring came, and the summer, and events followed in their appointed sequence, Craig and Diana continued to endure their happy marriage. She bought him a powerful gel to remove the hair on his heavily forested back, but she wouldn't apply it herself, he couldn't reach, and they let the matter slide. The daughters survived, thrived, learned from a few divorces. Craig still writes love notes to Diana and hides them, like Easter eggs, in places she doesn't expect. "You are my song and my prayer, you are a completion and a fulfillment, you are my angel huntress forever and ever . . ."

Spouse, surprised anew, even moved, sometimes replies in her own way: "Ditto."

That phrase "forever and ever" is a lyrical exaggeration, for in this world, nothing made of flesh is forever. Not even the giant centuries-old tortoises of Galápagos, sluggish though they may be. Not even the coral reefs and many minerals, which are not made of flesh. As to spirit, the question is still widely debated.

11

Still Alive: But All in Good Time, Might Not Be

For nine months I swam like a tiny fish in my mother, then was born and did my best to take over the lives of my parents. Firstborn son, I ruled. Later, I watched them fading, dying. In turn, I co-created my own little fish, five of them, and now they accompany me through the process of late living, future dying. I still feel like a fish swimming — not in my mother but free in the ocean. My eldest daughter tells me she doesn't like my living alone. I'm not alone! But much of my company is now invisible because only remembered.

One friend, call him Buddy, still survives from my childhood in Lakewood, Ohio. Inheriting from his parents, he lives in the same house where we ate buttered white Wonder Bread toast after school and pretended we weren't classroom rivals in addition to friends. At my family's house a few blocks away, we ate my mother's "sugarless" oatmeal raisin cookies. Because she said they were sugarless, they wouldn't harm our teeth. In those days, saying would make it so.

"Sugarless" did not mean there was no sugar in the cookies. "You wouldn't have wanted hardened bread, would you?" she explained sixty-five years later, clearing her con-science before she died. In our family we say "died" because we don't believe people go anyplace after death. Buddy's par-ents "passed on" years ago. We're both orphans now.

Buddy says he doesn't travel because he likes to be al-ways within a few steps of his bathroom with all the requisite implements. He was remodeling another room in his house, the Library, which had been installed by his upward-mobile parents. Exhibited on the shelves had been a blue glass Shirley Temple cream pitcher (a valuable "collectible" earned in a Kellogg's or Post Toasties promotion), a teakwood Buddha from the opening of a Chinese restaurant with its rival, a grinning plastic Confucius, stationed nearby (Buddy's family liked dining out on chop suey, chow mein, egg foo yung), trophies from travels and marksmanship competitions, and also a collection of books, including a Tarzan series from Buddy's childhood, the World Book encyclopedia set, and two of my novels.

Soon, when the contractor had finished removing the dark panels and shelves, the Library would be a den.

"A den?"

"A den, a den, a den," he said rapidly. "My Entertain-ment Center, plasma screen, the Japanese've come up with some real advances."

"Couldn't you just keep it as a library — ?"

"You think I have time to reread those old books with all the good shows out there, plus cable, plus my DVDs?"

"You used to . . . Remember in the summer we'd read a book a day and keep score?"

"I'm not so fond of reading lately. Maybe it's the

macular whatchacallit. I've got this macular generation, plus working my way from cataract to cardiac. And I could tell you about my prostrate — oh boy. But otherwise I'm mostly fine. My den remodel'll give me a leash on life."

I imagined him as an old dog on a new leash. I said, "We used to give ourselves names from Thomas Wolfe, James Branch Cabell, Kenneth Roberts —"

"Hey, I remember those days. The world was our oyster, right. But lately Bonnie did the reading, specially in our sunset years."

He fell silent. I said nothing, thinking this was the way to respect his silence, but after a while, I said, "You miss her?"

"Sometimes, yeah." He sighed and cast his eyes toward the contractor's unfinished work, the dark wood stacked in a corner. "Her birthday maybe. Other holidays. I'm gonna keep the ashes on that one shelf up there above my Entertainment Center. With the DVDs."

Buddy's teeth were regular and white, but not thanks to my mother's sugarless cookies. They were removable. He smiled as he used to. He didn't want me to think he was complaining. He said I was welcome anytime when I wanted to see how the Lakewood of our childhood had grown up and joined the real world of Cleveland.

Facetiousness is a poor but serviceable substitute for humor. When invited out, I often accept with gratitude, adding the ritual bit of graciousness that I have no social life and mostly can be found eating the Early Bird Special at Zim's, a chain restaurant, reading a newspaper, and using nail scissors to clip items that might come in handy someday, such as Health Advances or Grooming Tips for Seniors.

An uncomfortable ha-ha is the usual response. The generous host or hostess does not rescind the invitation.

In the traveling carnivals of my runaway adolescence, this was known as kidding on the square, but in fact, I do spend most evenings alone. It's true in the same sense that occasional bursts of talkativeness are only a way to camouflage my crippling stammer, stutter, and secret inarticulateness. A willingness to pick up conversations with fellow passengers on the bus is a means to hide shyness. As Walt Whitman would say if he were a contemporary adolescent, I contain multitudes of whatever.

So perhaps I'm only hiding encroaching senility by remembering the past and anticipating the future with relish as a screen for the inner drooling, limping, shrunken, bent, squeaking Herb.

Every year or so, I telephone my first college girlfriend and give thanks that her voice is still strong and clear, although she gives me news of the debilitation of her husband. We share unease at our changed worlds. Occasionally I also hear from a playmate of very early childhood, writing from her retirement home in South Carolina and begging me to accept Jesus before it's too late. Out of old friendship, remembering graham crackers and milk together on her parents' front porch, she wants to die knowing that I will not burn in hell. I don't have the heart to remind her that at age four we also used to play Hospital together, a game made in heaven for us because I had no sisters and she had no brothers and therefore we were both intensely curious about the

anatomy of the opposite and, frequently, opposing sex. On a
need-to-know basis, she doesn't need this reminder after her
long life of evangelical piety.

I began to read the obituary pages because of what I told
myself was an interest in stories, each obituary representing a
condensed life, although too many of them seemed to be the
story of an insurance company vice president's career. Then I
began to notice that some of them, more of them, many of
the defunct were my age ("So young," I would mouth aloud).
Now I still think, So Young, although most of the perishing
renowned who earn lead obituaries in *The New York Times*
are younger than I am, veterans of later wars than mine.

I pay close attention to the mini-stories that indicate a
second or third spouse, sometimes taken at an advanced age.
Good for you, I decide over a favorite vegetable and bean
curd dish at my neighborhood Chinese restaurant (adequate
light for reading, nice Yolanda my regular waitress).

I regret the loss of enemies, too. Like friends, beloveds,
and the famous, the hated fill a place in our hearts. On the
one ghoulish hand, I grieve for their consequent inability to
repent. On the other, dripping with gore and black with
spite, I lose with the death of an enemy the ability to take revenge. What's the use of hatred now? The philosopher Irwin
Corey taught me that without hatred, there can be no joy in
revenge.

What is happening with these losses is a gradual depop-
ulation of my world. I don't want to become the goofy old
guy heading out for coffee with the morning newspaper under his arm and his head filled with nothing but nostalgia,
which, like jealousy, does no good work and produces dimin-

ishing returns. History should be a continuing activity, leading into the future.

When I hike, sometimes there's a sudden shooting pain in my right foot that comes and goes without warning. If it's too intense, I stop, but usually I just keep on walking and it mysteriously disappears. My doctor can't find a cause. I used to jump off towers in the Army to prepare for parachuting into the perhaps welcoming arms of our gallant Soviet allies. It was wartime and doctors had the convenient notion of treating severe sprains by injecting morphine into the foot and ankle, binding them, and then sending the soldier (me) back to duty. I wonder if this present pain is a shadow memory of an injury from more than sixty years ago. Just as I did in the Army, I'll live with it; walk, run, and jump through it.

Fascinated all my adult life by Haiti, that isolato of nations, I've been returning gratefully to the scene of familiar crimes and joys since 1953. Haiti is a tragedy you can dance to. My first marriage decayed dramatically on a chaotic tropical island among its songs and ceremonies. On a treasure hunt I joined a group of Haitian friends with a pirate map. In the north of Hispaniola, opposite the Île de la Tortue, in the village of Port-de-Paix, I found not Spanish doubloons but malaria. Anopheles bit me one night when a girl whispered from the road and I opened the shutters to joke with her. She said she wanted to know if I was white all over.

I took other risks during the steady crescendo of Haitian political disasters. *Chimères, tontons macoutes*, attachés, sometimes even official uniformed thugs, serving the successive dictators, harassed unwelcome visitors. Any individual Haitian is an angel, a friend says, but any group of Haitians is a mob. I was a young student there, I was a nosy journalist, I am a fanatic older guy haunted by memories. My son Ethan says I'm seeing ghosts. Until I stop seeing them, I'm still a would-be writer anticipating imminent festivals. I ask Ethan to allow a father his nostalgia. I can remember the past and, when lonely, populate the present with those ghosts. The supply never diminishes.

Each time I arrive at the grandiosely named Port-au-Prince International Airport, no longer greeted by merengue bands playing "Haïti Chérie" in the current days of no tourists and bottomless desolation, I somehow become young again despite, despite . . . I've been infected with the music, the language, the art, and the past. Hans Christoph Buch, a German writer who has also been infected with the malady of Haiti-fascination, tells about an old friend who awoke in her house to hear a thief stealthily moving about. She screamed in Creole, "Who's there?" and he answered, "It's the thief, Madame." "Get out of here!" "Just a moment, Madame, I haven't quite finished."

Now the thieves carry guns and use them. Cuteness has evaporated. Misery is nearly complete. There seems, in fact, to be little hope for Haiti. There is still a heartrending yearning and stoical desperation; there are, for me, old friends, a history, those ghosts.

Two of my remaining friends from that first long stay, during what Haitians now call "the golden age" — General Magloire's brutality was casual, irregular, drunken, and merely greedy — died in 2001. I wonder who will be next. Three years ago, my son Ari held me up to help me breathe after I had eaten algae-poisoned *lambi*, a Caribbean shellfish presently to be avoided. Haitian beaches don't post warning signs during the red tide season. They don't post warning signs about much of anything, although risks to life are not unknown.

I fainted on the lovely gingerbread terrace of the Hotel Oloffson and half woke to find waiters and a friend depositing me in my bed, where I lay for a few days, concentrating on breathing. Ari slept in another bed alongside. One night when I fell into a state of semiparalysis, hiccupping, he held me up, seeming calm, and kept asking me to take a breath. I did so. Finally I said, "Okay, okay, I'm okay," and lay back against the musty pillow, which had known many heads before mine. It felt so good, I was so happy just to breathe and to think about nothing else in the entire world except gratitude for this first son, watching over me.

That night could be taken as a hint of things to come. But I miss the sweetness of the flesh of lambi, a shellfish something like abalone, doubly unkosher now. It's another loss to add to my stock of them.

That poisoned lambi brings continual pleasure into my life. It gives me the memory of Ari calmly watching. I'll never be alone in this world. Like Polonius, I try to pass on to my children some scrappy knowledge I think I've accumulated; the blessing of their existence is a wisdom they pass on to me.

Youth may be wasted on the young, but agedness is also wasted on the old, who are often too preoccupied lining up their time-release pills to relax and really enjoy their diminishment. Time-release also applies to bodies and souls, even in those who think it doesn't. I'll never sit in an undershirt over a microwaved supper in a lonely kitchen. Even if I did, it wouldn't be illuminated by a bare bulb as I read the newspaper, lips moving, using a nail clipper to cut more pieces of the paper to send to faraway and uncaring children. (I would have misplaced the scissors and put them in the freezer.) I do clip things, of course, but in a Starbucks where the light is better. And my compassionate offspring claim to be amused by my notes in the margins. I know where the scissors are.

Also don't wear a senior bus pass on a shoelace around my neck. Keep my driver's license current.

About Haiti, about my two marriages (one bad, one good, both ended), about my disappeared friends, I think I remember everything, although there's a tendency to selectivity — remember more of the bad about the bad marriage, more of the good about the good one. Anarchy would reign if we remembered everything; it would be a senseless collage. I still have words to try to put the recollections in some kind of order. That wife I loved, she also loved me, she stopped loving me, she went on to another life, she died. So it was.

Judging by standard insurance statistics, I'm too old to be even a *retired* policeman. Years ago, I wrote a poem for the wife I loved to mark my fiftieth birthday, telling her, *Young Wife, now I'm old enough to be a Responsible Negro Leader*, although I didn't carry the Reverend Al Sharptonesque belly or skin color. So why now, more than thirty years later, after that wife I loved stopped loving me, do I feel too young to give up poking into other people's business? I stare at crazies in the street, also at pretty young women; I say, "Thank you for sharing the sordid details of your life" to cell phone blabbers in cafés and on buses. I would look for a forty-year mortgage if I found a new young wife to join me. I terrify my children with the threat.

In the morning, in the cafés where I insult the loud cell phone blabbers, I replenish my stock of disasters by reading *The New York Times* and the *San Francisco Chronicle*. The ever-new, ever-deepening chaos of Haiti is a long-running obituary notice. Even before I check the front page, I turn to the more personal obituary notices, looking for friends and enemies, but so far have been able, usually, to skip the small-type paid announcements. I prefer to appear on the termite-supported wooden terrace of the Hotel Oloffson in Port-au-Prince, not in the obituaries. Maybe I'll honeymoon there with an as-yet-undiscovered wife whom my children will have to deal with.

I've given up asking Pamela Fiori, editor of *Town & Country*, to appoint me chief of their Port-au-Prince bureau. *Town & Country* magazine can't use a profile of the most distinguished cocaine dealer in Pétionville or a sparkling evocation of the seaside country club for MREs, the Morally Repugnant Elite, and the Bon Ton Macoutes just off the road to Saint-Marc. I try to entertain Pamela with the suggestion, but it seems to make her nervous.

She buys me a nice lunch in Manhattan anyway. A shellfish pasta without red tide algae is just the right accompaniment for a proposal by the veteran wordguy to explore "Haiti, Fun in the Sun." She hesitates, then asks if I want dessert.

Amid its chaos, I still feel alive and energetic in Haiti. Cockcrow still wakes me at dawn. Even if I'm dreaming of an unrecoverable past — treasure hunt with an improbable treasure map, laughter and dancing, many rum-sodas during the tropical destruction of a marriage — that past is still in my possession. It's secure in the vault of memory. What happened then surely can't happen again, but something else might.

Who am I to give up possibility? Something else always does happen.

Some of the dead have children in Haiti. Sheelagh has a daughter, Jean has a son, Issa has a daughter and a son, Aubelin has many. My old friends are present despite their absence.

A doctor pal in San Francisco eats very slowly, seeming to stop the world while he lifts his fork, glaring at it. Since we have always shared our stories, we talk about a familiar topic. The fork arrives at his mouth. He continues: "I met this nice person —"

I watch the fork begin the redescent to his plate. He is still balefully studying it.

"Do you like her? Is it love?"

He twirls and twirls. A few strands of pasta cling to the slowly revolving fork. He sighs. "I'm not ready to settle down again. Been there, done that."

The fork rises. He stares. I don't ask if he thinks the food might attack him. A tomato-affiliated pasta strand falls onto his shirt. He shrugs. "I wasn't paying attention."

I nod at the explanation. He has a right to it. Parkinsonism is not easy to conceal. His thumb and some of his fingers are jumping as he puts his hand in his lap. He will not marry again. He will not rush food to his mouth. He will do his best not to drop his fork. He won't practice surgery, but he will hide the shaking and stiffness as long as he can.

It's unlikely that an illustrated manual entitled *The Joys of Decrepitude* would find a grateful audience among folks seeking a gift for Grandparents Day. The comedy of falling apart or self-help hardcovers with accompanying CD, *Let's Get Debilitated!* complete with a translation for the early-stage Alzheimer'd (that means Old) will not appeal to publishers. *The Joy of Sex* was illustrated with drawings of isometric riffs and variations. Few would relish photos or sketches of novel constipation-easing postures, nor will the makers of Depends, stool softeners, and denture cleansers rush to advertise in *Naptime, The Journal for Sunset Couples.*

Another contemporary, a singer, has decided on a change of careers. "Always kind of wanted to act, so why not? Character parts, probably."

"You present yourself well," I say, and it's the truth. "You always have."

He grins appreciatively. He senses sincerity. "Comedy probably, maybe use my singing, too. Combine things, am I right?"

And then, because we've been friends forever, or at least since we called ourselves "the dynamic duo" — a writer and a singer in college days — I offer him a silent nod.

"Okay, pal, I'm not leveling with you because you already know, so we can't call it leveling. Can't hack it anymore. Don't have the breath, the volume, the range is gone."

I tell him thanks. Tell him I have problems, too. Tell him my problems, some of them anyway, the main one being anticipation. In our different ways, we're working toward the same conclusion, which does not involve singing or writing. We wish to sing or write along the way until we get there. "Eventually, maybe in a year or so, I can be cast as First Dead Man in a show about undertakers," he says. "I've got a great future in mortuary dramas."

"That's so last season." I suggest he should audition for a part in the next big biblical movie, *Armageddon: The Sequel*, starring Angelina Jolie in the title role, as Arma.

We're not ready to cry the end of the world, despite a big evangelical market for it. Arma will save us. The public festival of comedy and tragedy makes us want to get out of bed in the morning. Street madness is an essential ingredient (get out of our apartments, too). If I'm not answering the phone, dear daughter Ann, it doesn't necessarily mean I'm lying there helpless with a stroke. I'm someplace in the carnival, wandering down the midway.

And suddenly my friend and colleague in the survival trade breaks into the first lines of an aria from *Boris Godunov*: "I am dying. Six years now I have ruled all alone . . ." In the opera, he only reigns for six years, but in life, we can rule for more. My friend, the singer, and I are trying to learn that even in real life there are limits.

In old age we treasure life because, by God, we still have it, and suffer suspicion of life because it fails us and we are losing it. We take pride in our history; we see our past dreams and striving as futile. Probably there are as many ways to be old as there are old folks practicing the game. I still remember Miss Collins, my teacher at Taft Elementary School in Lakewood, Ohio, who touched my head indulgently, impatiently, tenderly, as I stood in line at the drinking fountain: "That was nice work. But you misspelled 'gruesome.'" I had written a "grewsome" story. Her praise thrilled me; her criticism made me want to work harder.

She stroked my hair! Perhaps, more than seventy years later, I still write to please Miss Collins.

She looked at the clock in the hall and added, "It's getting late. Time for milk and cookies. Go home."

I still write for Miss Collins, my friend Marvin, my brother Sid, and the girl, now an evangelical in her assisted living complex in South Carolina, with whom I played Hospital.

Life as an Older Young Writer

"Hi, Herb! Still writing?"

Writers should get used to the idea that some people are under the well-intended illusion that tellers of stories resemble human beings. Writers can't serve thirty years and then earn release to play golf, wear a baseball cap, entertain themselves by negotiating shopping carts down the aisles of the local supermarket. A writer might rest, brood, stir uneasily, drink too much, chase persons of the same or the opposite sex, but he or she is always on the lookout for the next book. Waits. Doesn't retire. Unless . . .

"Hi, how've you been? Still writing?"

"Do I look as if I have Alzheimer's?" This response helps to explain why I have few living friends and even acquaintances are falling away. Sometimes I try to be agreeable, or at least less snotty, and explain that only normal folks retire. Writers might despair or suffer writer's block, usually loudly, but they don't decide to quit unless they are even more disturbed than they had to be in order to become writers in the first place.

Still writing? With reluctant compassion, I try to salve the lady's feelings. After all, I want her to have friendly memories when I am finally, inevitably, "in the course of human events," gone, finished, not invited to receptions or fundraisers anymore — "passed on." I explain: "Writers want to do it. They need it. They don't willingly stop. There's no retirement. May I get you a glass of chardonnay?"

But then, instead of trotting off nicely, lyingly, for her wine, and probably not returning, I continue the conversation. "You know" — but she doesn't know — "golf, bridge, cruises where you stop in exotic tropical places to buy T-shirts for your grandchildren, are . . ." Suddenly I recall the words for "compassion" in several languages and don't add the words "boring" or "stupid." Instead, I say, "Kids hate it when they have to give you a kiss in return for the T-shirt. Was that white or red you wanted?"

"*My* grandchildren don't mind," she says.

When I was in my twenties, I used as the epigraph for a novel, *The Man Who Was Not With It*, lines from a poem by Rimbaud: "It should be every man's ambition to be his own doctor." As time rolled on, it turned out that this ambition was not to be realized by either Rimbaud or me. I have consulted doctors; I receive Medicare. Now I need another poet to write that every person should learn to overcome the melancholy of age. And how should a person do this? Here is a suggested course of action. By not being melancholic, by avoiding sadness, by overcoming grief. And also by wading through and out of the swamp of dulled feelings.

Not so easy; I've lost my way a few times. The world is very much with us. One rumor — that death is inevitable — happens to be true.

When she learned that I lacked medical insurance, my eldest daughter protested angrily. "I'm healthy," I explained. "But you need insurance anyway," she counterexplained. "Don't nag, I keep a cyanide tablet in my mouth and I'll bite down if there's danger that your inheritance is at risk," I counter-counterexplained. "Dad!" she cried. This is a daughter's unanswerable weapon, pronounced *Daa*-aad.

Fortunately, Medicare checked in. Peace reigns in the family. Death is not imminent. I've let the cyanide Use-By date expire.

On some days, inclement weather not necessarily the determinant, life seems to be over. The internal thermostat just shuts off. Maybe the liver is slow to do its work or the cloaca or the brain clotted with static. I imagine looks of indulgence from neighbors as the codger trudges up the steps of the hill where I live. A spy at a window may be thinking: He can still climb, but shouldn't he stop to rest? Looks like he should.

This window on Russian Hill in San Francisco is the one I ran past many years ago and saw a miniskirted beauty doing the Twist with her boyfriend on a late summer afternoon. I vowed to replace him and, briefly, did. I don't recall her name anymore, but she is very possibly a grandmother in El Cerrito. I still live on Russian Hill and have tallied various inhabitants of that house — a Chinese woman who scraped the moss from the steps with a spoon, a couple of dot-com yuppies who moved on to build their dream house in Atherton, an architect who listened to my history of the building with impatient bemusement. I spoke with the neighbors even before I earned the right to their indulgence.

Once upon a time I was a teenager, being trained by the U.S. Army to speak Russian (*Soviet* Russian) and preparing to jump out of airplanes to greet our gallant Soviet allies. "I am your friend! I am an American soldier and your friend!" It was important to announce this quickly in order to avoid being shot; I still remember the Russian words. My duty was to explain how to use American equipment. I no longer remember the Russian words for the parts of the Browning automatic rifle, although sometimes they float into my dreams. (When I wake, sometimes I can't even remember the more recent birth names of Snoop Dogg or Eminem; age-related inefficiency.) I can still feel the chill of Camp Ritchie, the military intelligence training center where I graduated in the twenty-second class; I smell the snow (*sneg*) and the Maryland winter apple orchards (*yabloka* means "apple" in Russian); I remember trying to orient myself with a Russian map showing a Baptist church (*tserkov*). Occasionally I meet another Ritchie graduate, and we report to each other that the base is long demolished but rumored now to lie above a secret underground alternative Pentagon. After the atomic surprise attack, please direct your Medicare inquiries to: Below Camp Ritchie, Maryland.

On our weekend passes, the Ritchie boys went to Baltimore to buy black bread in the market, drink beer, and chase girls to whom we would hint darkly that we were doing secret work. When a young woman quite reasonably dumped me for an Air Force officer with a tailored uniform, I consoled myself with a complete Shakespeare in Russian, which I had found in a used bookstore. The tailored Air Force officer probably couldn't recite much of "*Bit eeli nyeh bit, vot takoi vopros* . . . To be or not to be, that is the question."

But then, probably he had the consolation of getting laid.

Well, if he's still alive, he may remember the Peabody Bookshop beauty's name, just as I remember that icy winter in Baltimore when we both were, and in memory still are, but one day will not be. I look forward to not recognizing him if we happen to be among the final stragglers at a last convention in Saratoga Springs.

"You look terrific!" I say to my fellow Ritchie boy.

"Haven't changed a bit, have I?" he answers. And peers at my face through his bifocals to see if, like Pinocchio's, my nose has grown longer.

The life-affirming joys of hatred and revenge invigorate a person like a surge of steroids, but with age, the purity of passion can be disturbed by double vision. (The hated one is contemptible, and yet . . . He deserves nothing but spite, but hold on now.) Therefore I obeyed the peculiar impulse to invite a former, *seriously* former friend to meet me at the Chameleon Cafe in my neighborhood.

It was an inspiration that didn't rise to the level of a considered idea because it couldn't change my mind about the former friend's status. But it seemed like time to indulge whims — a gambling weekend in Las Vegas, an overdose of sweet barbecue, a beveraging hour with a cheating, lying, conniving, remorseless sleazebag. For whom I no longer had fond feelings.

Extant was a grievance about a financial scam. I used to host a dinner for other victims on the anniversary of the futile legal decision in our favor. Each year I would invite as a

Special Surprise Attraction someone who had been similarly afflicted by the same affable and charming operator; we would laugh, applaud, and toast the guest star as he recounted his adventure, sometimes breaking glasses in our enthusiasm.

A doctor, cheated by the same pal, used to stand at the pool where they both swam, shouting: "You're polluting the water! Get out of the pool!"

This disturbed the meditative Zen stillness, which even a thief enjoys while doing his laps. He switched health clubs. Despite my own complaints, I thought our doctor colleague was going too far. In California, routines of physical fitness are sacred, like the marriage bed in other cultures.

At the afternoon date with my former friend, I bought the lattes and organic bran muffins. After all, I was the host. It was only right. He looked haggard and shrunken, going through a serious divorce. He had married the lady at the time of our lawsuit and put most of his assets in her name, protecting them from his victims. (Perhaps she was also his type.) During the settlement conference, when his lawyer explained the situation, I considered expressing my opinion in the matter with the famous booger-flick — a finger to one's nose, which then skillfully projects its moist accumulation at the adversary. More eloquently than words, this could enhance understanding of diminished regard for my former friend.

Now he brightened with pleasure at the assumption that I had "put our little business disagreement behind us." He made a tearing-paper, casting-out gesture.

I said that I was sorry about all the trouble in his life. His back, his knees, osteoporosis, divorce, child custody, asset division, all that must be difficult for him. On my next trip to

Haiti — compassion flooding my soul — I might visit the voodoo priest who had put a curse upon his existence. I might ask him to remove it. I might also extract the pins I had inserted in the back, knees, and genitals of the dedicated *ouanga*, the black magic doll, I had hung in my closet.

I might do so if it was not too expensive to cancel a Haitian *fatwa*. Options need to be weighed; commitments shouldn't be made lightly. But after all, I had pleasant memories of tennis and abalone diving. I was hoping this erosion of my temper did not signal any ominous softening of my heart. Compassion is desirable, forgiveness is a virtue respected in many creeds, but betrayal of friendship for mere dollars still seemed drastically discourteous. I told him I prayed events would look up for him in the distant future. That was a slip of the tongue; I meant to say near future.

"How's it going?"

"Not so . . . not so okay."

"Things will improve," I warmly replied, not going into detail about whether things would improve for him or for the efficiency of my voodoo priest.

"Gee, thanks."

"It's nothing." But in fact, it was something. I decided at that moment to remove the pins from the *ouanga* in that dark corner behind the all-cotton Banana Republic shirts. (These pins also bring migraines, bad breath, poverty, and parking tickets.) Maybe in a month or two, if I happened to be packing tropical clothes for my next trip to Haiti, I'd take a look at the thickly-stuck *ouanga*.

And yet, and yet, hearing him reminisce about our old companionship, I too felt sentiment welling in me. We used to drive to Big Sur together, we pulled on wet suits and pried abalone off rocks when it was approximately legal, we pursued the bachelor life together, we discussed taking or not taking mind-expanding cactus brews. It was the sixties, after all.

I also planned to tell him, as we picked at the raisins fallen from our bran muffins, that I no longer bore him any resentment. He had taught me something about human nature — that it was not to be trusted. Red in tooth and claw; nasty, brutish, and now short; only about five feet seven, in fact, due to calcium loss. But I couldn't speak these things aloud. Anyway, he was not a regular reader of Hobbes or Machiavelli. He was a human creature with a cheerful relish in his hustle through the city. My intelligent second wife used to suggest I try looking at him by the fluorescence of the Safeway meat counter, a glow that she claimed would strip away the jolly surface to reveal inner character.

Only when his excess of grateful, damp-eyed feeling overflowed as we said good-bye did it occur to me to say: Wait now. Sit down again. You're a schmuck. I want to remind you of that.

I let the impulse pass. Bile brings acid reflux, a lasting aftertaste. So thank you, old pal. You enriched my life.

Next time, he said, the snack would be on him. Knowing I was watching, he jumped into his antique Mercedes 280 SL convertible — top rakishly folded down despite the fog — just as he used to, barely wincing because of his arthritis. He waved a happy salute.

As de Gaulle wrote, Old age is a shipwreck. But not necessarily. It can be a holiday in truly liberated reality after the vain, anything-is-possible fantasies of youth. Blonds may have

more fun, but grays have more responsibilities. As an eighteen-year-old soldier, I was convinced nothing could kill me.
Now I'm not so sure. I wasn't afraid of jumping out of airplanes; now I get vertigo at the edge of a roof. Evidence of
the slippery slope surrounds me. I need my rest and look forward to a nap after lunch — a power nap, of course.

There are hours of gray dreariness as I think of the
friends summoned away, one by one: Paul, George, Bernard
(two Bernards), Bob, Anatole, Gavin, Rex, Saul (two Sauls,
also), Ed, Marvin (long ago in the war), Issa, Ted, and surely
tonight I will wake suddenly to remember others. Aubelin,
Dwight, Max, Alan (two Alans), Albert — I don't have to
wait for the middle of the night for these specters to rise up.
Those who introduced me to new ideas, those who confessed
their ambitions, failures, and longings and to whom I confessed mine, some who were merely good company because
we laughed a lot together, but surely that's not a *merely*. I'll
not list the women because the list doesn't need a complete
inventory of griefs and lonelinesses. Ben, Jacques, Roland . . .
No, I'll stop. I've learned to go to the movies and to hike
alone; it's harder to learn to laugh alone.

Scrapbooks, photo albums, letters in boxes, journals, become instruments for nostalgia and pain. Perhaps they help to
deal with reality, just as does the dentist's drill, but unlike the
dentist's drill, they excavate but do not clear away. The sharp-
ness of immediate grief, that stab of acknowledgment, is part
of life we have to live; prolonged useless yearning, like jealousy, is a condition that does no work.

In fact, of course, I don't want to lose the memories and
reminders of those who are gone. I had better accept the excess life given me with gratitude. The alternatives, such as a

career of mourning, wastes the times past with those cherished ones.

A friend complains of unusual memory loss, as opposed to the usual kinds. I'll not use his name, although I remember it. Many of my contemporaries speak more of what they have given up than of the futures they plan. Joint problems are noted as things to live with, not to repair. I miss playing tennis or racquetball with partners who used to be better and tougher than I was. Drastic stress on the spine is out of the question, covering four walls or rushing the net. Most of my cohorts no longer travel with sleeping bags.

I too complain. I'm not ill (knock on wood), but suffer loneliness as the ranks thin. Why should anyone sympathize with me? Looking on the bright side, if it's eventually a contest, say, between cancer and me, even if I don't win, at least I can come in second.

Awakening to death, a kind of prememory of "the distinguished thing" to come, helps to appreciate the life we have now. The passage of seasons gives both sadness and pleasure; fall's muted colors are as touching as springtime's bright and gleaming ones.

Some people, of course, believe in an afterlife, like a movie remake or sequel. Memory passed along is the best afterlife to dream of. There's enough loveliness in the sky — nightglow and daybright, clouds, sun, stars, planets — without angels and ghosts cluttering things up. Our duty (in my opinion; excuse me) is to create the closest approximation we can to heaven here below, while we are here, although the human race so far has not proven to be very good at it. Room for improvement gives us something to live for.

When a friend asked Saul Bellow, recuperating from an

illness but sick and old, if he was getting better, he answered: "I've been getting better my whole life. Now just look where it's got me."

I Was So Much Younger Then
(An Old Story)

Proust, at the end of his monster effort to recover lost time, and by doing so, to redeem it, tells of venturing out of his cork-lined present to a party where he hopes to meet again the friends of his past. Instead, he enters a nightmarish scene of garish crones, doddering relics, desiccated and lumpy masks of themselves. Dwelling as he did in time past, this exemplified Freud's definition of the uncanny: something which cannot be, *cannot*, and yet is. Marcel is horrified.

Then he notices a young woman. He speaks to her. He sees in her eyes her reflexive disdain: *Who is this geezer?* And realizes what he has become.

In a North Beach coffeehouse, I take a table near a skinny California beauty with the just slight loosening at the belly, which healthy skinny California yoga practitioners offer as part of their blessing upon the universe. She is reading a book in French with a pocket dictionary by her side. Ah, but life is beautiful! (And also, *la vie est belle*.) I can always chat up a woman who reads French.

My plan, eventually, if all begins well, if her fluency is sufficient, is to point out with sophisticated *savoir-vivre* that I am definitely of another generation, in case she wondered. And if I were twenty years younger, a relationship between us would still be inappropriate. But since I am even beyond the twenty-year cutoff date, our relationship would be ludicrous. Therefore (raising a Sorbonne-trained Gallic finger on behalf of close attention) all she needs about the situation is a sense of humor and we're in business.

What decent café reader of French could resist this appeal?

But before I advance to the envisioned triumphal conclusion, I notice in her eyes a certain look: *This guy seems harmless . . . maybe a professor or something . . . Whatever.*

At least old Chinese ladies don't get up to offer me their seats on crowded buses; not yet.

Now I'm explaining to the Francophile in the café that I'm a skopto-klepto-bibliophiliac, pronouncing it slowly to see if the light of interest can be kindled. "It's a word I made up. It means a person who likes to steal looks at other people's books."

She doesn't say, "In that case, *Franco*-skopto-klepto-biblio . . ."

She says, "So you used to teach French before you retired?"

Like some older guys, I wake in the morning young, virile, and filled with hope. After good nights. Sometimes. Forgetting the middle-of-the-night call to bathroom duty, where the body's business is accompanied by past losses and fear that sleep will now desert us.

On the less good nights, I glance in passing at the unfamiliar grizzled head in the mirror. I lie awake till dawn, listening for the first chirpings of the robins and sparrows of my childhood. I don't hear them because the birds have disappeared, or because the little ear cilia that conduct sound toward the brain are now sparse and shriveled, thanks to gunfire, rock 'n' roll, and time.

Or I manage to return to sleep and dream of the lost wife who in memory still takes my arm like a happy lover. I wake and dismiss the three A.M. insomnia as vain and self-indulgent. I do some stretches, leg lifts, and pushups on a mat. I follow the routines of cold water on my face, a brisk stroll, coffee amid the anonymous good-fellowship of a public place. For once more I am young, virile, and filled with hope.

Who was that man in the mirror? What is the grizzled beard doing on a face like that of my father? These are old questions, this is an old story. Those who plan to live long had better deal with a plan for answering the questions, but of course they won't. As a by-product of youth, we knew ourselves to be immortal. Once I jumped out of an airplane and asked the captain on the ground why, obeying our training, I had to kick the soldier on the stick ahead of me to get him out. "He's twenty-eight," said the captain. I was nineteen.

Instead of sleeping forever, or even till ten in the morning, I still rise and shine, which was the command of training sergeants in that war whose veterans are diminishing in number by the thousands each day: "Rise and shine, assholes!"

In 1956 I spent a summer in retreat from the desolate early marriage at an artist's refuge near Saratoga, New York. I ate well, whined to my companions, fellow strivers, listened over and over to a Louis Armstrong recording that I recall as "Loveless Love," but was actually a version of "Careless Love." Louis Armstrong's thick happy articulation was a great comfort. Loud complaint appealed to me. I hit my Olivetti Lettera 32 portable typewriter with my pains.

Pouring words over trouble sometimes calms, sometimes adds gunpowder to the fire. Rehearsing rage, inventing, elaborating, remembering idiocies, remembering regret, blaming another, blaming myself, pleading, denouncing, sorting out, muddling, telling a story was fulfilling and exhausting. Telling this story was a moral aerobic exercise. "Loveless Love" rumbled and growled in my head. Moral aerobic exercise doesn't necessarily bring the sleep of the just or any other variety of peace. I had nightmares despite telling myself that self-pity was about as useless as jealousy. Love oh love oh loveless love.

It was hard work to master a dilemma that was the opposite of the pain a young Mick Jagger snarled and sang about ten years later. Sometimes you can't even get what you *don't* want.

Late in my term at this retreat, it dawned on me that we were guests, not inmates. I decided to walk into town like a normal decent person, carrying money in my pocket in case options for spending it presented themselves (beer, cheeseburger, postcards). There would be strangers in Saratoga Springs, tourists and summer visitors. I would amble among them like a living creature in a place of non-complainers. It was a pleasant hike to a main street with ramshackle but grand hotels, built with spacious terraces, from the days when folks came to take the waters at the spa.

And the sight terrified me — a nightmare vision of an entire population brought down by a curse. Everybody here was ancient. I had not left the grounds of Yaddo for nearly two months while the world had sunk into decrepitude. Wheelchairs, crutches, rolling walkers, gaped mouths, a drifting crowd of the drooling and the crippled filled the street.

They were strewn on the verandas like the debris of some magic catastrophe. Quick, I needed a mirror. I was sure also to be one of these palsied, shrunken, pitiful creatures taking lurching or shuffling steps if they walked at all, making little mouse snorts with the effort.

Then I saw the banner stretched above the street: WELCOME VETERANS OF THE SPANISH-AMERICAN WAR. It may have been their last convention.

Thanks to abated panic, I then noticed attendants, children, grandchildren, watching over the veterans. There were a few sturdy younger wives, too. The heroes of the "Remember the Maine" war were not throwing water-filled balloons and condoms like the veterans of my war. They were back-bent, slumped, mostly three- or four-legged if ambulatory. There were kindly and patient expressions on the faces of those pushing wheelchairs. I already knew the word "Parkinson's" and in due course would learn the word "Alzheimer's." Even today, there could be a bureau in Washington, where nothing ever quite dies, with a clerk in charge of disbursing final survivor pensions to the no-longer-young widow of a bugle boy from the Spanish-American War.

I was released from fear, I felt warm and alert in downtown Saratoga. I found a tavern for a beer and a hamburger. I noticed a pretty young woman, probably a student at Skidmore College with a forged ID (*Where are you now, pretty young woman? Please write.*) I hiked back to Yaddo, ready to make a final copy of my story inspired by early romance, too-early marriage, and grief for the child victims of their parents.

★　　★　　★

The grammar of my future needs parsing. Who I will have been when I cease to be is the sum of what I was. It's a congeries of verb tenses, future, present, past, not to mention conditional.

Still leading this conditional existence, I visit my son Ari in New York, and we ride bikes up the trail along the West Side Highway. I'm entertained by his concern as he keeps glancing back to make sure I'm not wobbling into traffic. I feel a surge of happiness in the river breezes, on a bike, May in Manhattan; the big-city joys of the strollers in their jeans, the joggers, the other bicyclists sailing along. Ari grins, he winks. He is young, strong, filled with hope and ambition. At this moment, I too will live forever.

Later, when he meets me for dinner with his girlfriend, she does me the honor of not treating me as if I'm totally harmless. They bait me for reminiscing about times in the Village before herpes and AIDS. When they go off together (I say I'm sleepy), I decide to sit awhile at the White Horse Tavern, where Dylan Thomas took his last drink and where Norman Mailer, in 1958, in his alternating Irish brawler and Texas cowboy phases, told me he didn't like Israelis because they spoke Yiddish, that language of his childhood in Brooklyn. Either he didn't yet know that the language of Israel is Hebrew, or more likely, he was making the point about his adopted roles, or most likely, he was simply announcing that he lacked any interest in the concerns of the non-headbutting Jewish writer from Cleveland. It was the era of *Advertisements for Myself*. We've both outgrown that quarrel.

In recent years I also notice changes in my children. Ari kept glancing behind to see how I was managing as we bicycled; Ethan explained three times how to get to his apartment in Los Angeles; Ann telephones every day, and calls her siblings if she doesn't reach or hear from me within a few hours. Hey, Ari, is my bike wobbling? Ethan, do you expect me to wander in the City and County of Los Angeles until a kindly social worker leads me to you? Ann: What if something interesting is happening and I'm too busy to call? Judy hasn't yet reached the stage of adjusting pillows behind my head to make sure I'm comfy. Nina did, however, try to help me snap on a seatbelt.

I've passed the traditional cutoff point for elders and have no justification for persistence. Genes, vitamins, Haiti, children, a wife I loved and lost are on offer; maybe my father's grandfather, who according to family legend lived to be 122, is the culprit. He was said to pass his later years dangling money on a fishing line out of a second-story window and jerking it out of reach when passersby bent to pick it up, his cackles of laughter resounding down the street. I haven't yet bought my fishing equipment. Trying to teach others to nurture their old loves, hatreds, and ambitions is a mug's game, or a televangelist's. Balzac (maybe someone else) said that Paris is the paradise of misery and the capital of hope. Old age is something like this grand ancient city, a stalwart relic shared with the rest of the natural world. We begin in dust and end in dust, true; but . . . new rocks appear in the terraced mountain fields of Haiti, no matter how often the peasants clear them. In the ceaseless churning of the earth, fresh outcroppings grow out to replace the disappeared ones.

I can't reject old age. (I don't have a choice, do I?) Diligently observing the situation, I'll embrace it cautiously, tentatively, considering that it will not last forever. On the days of the Real Foods senior discount — it's Tuesday and Thursday, if you want to conserve resources — I tell the cashier I'm still eligible.

When Ann telephones to check on my welfare, I enjoy asking her if she would like me to take a healthy young wife to see to it that I'm not dangerously alone. The new wife could also make good use of the inheritance otherwise merely dissipated by children and grandchildren. "You want me to be happy, don't you, Ann? If she turns out to be a heavyweight drinker, hair colorer, and shopper, but she's nice to me and I have a stroke in her arms, wouldn't that be a pleasant way for your dad to go?"

Alexander Dumas' children used to listen at the bedroom door as their old father, the most famous French writer of his time, made love to a succession of respectful demoiselles. No prurient interest; they simply worried about his health. At a crucial moment, they heard one of the acolytes cry out in ecstasy, "Now, oh now, Monsieur le Dramaturge!"

Like my children, like everyone, I entered the world noisily, but most likely will go out in silence, nobody slapping my rump. Betweentimes, most of us do our best to stir things up in such a way that others — family, friends, lovers, even adversaries and enemies — accompany our departure with their thoughts. They make comments. They may be preoccupied for a time with our images. They glimpse reminders in the street, styles of walking or the familiar shape of a head. Flashbacks are evidence of our existence. Someone has a loving dream. Someone else dreams of revenge, waking to realize that it's too late for revenge, and hatred can bring no further satisfaction.

Gradually, the memory fades. Perhaps there's a pang like Buddy's on his wife's birthday. In some cases, there's a historical record, at least a stone or a plaque. The grave marker is what remains of most of us, not how we grinned at the smell of roast beef or touched a beloved with a yearning hand. Fortunately we're no longer in the neighborhood to notice how we have been forgotten. Staring into the time when I am gone is like standing near a crowded pool where I am forbidden to swim. Look, they're splashing and laughing! They're bumping and flirting! . . . But I'm behind thick glass, dreaming I could join them.

On good days I still wake to the beginning of life, expectations of crisp air, appetite, victories. The force that drives the red fuse through the body renews itself. I'm still alive, although those words echo the resigned beat of Tolstoy's last diaries, a nearly daily account of his dreadful quarrels with his wife, his final defeats and oncoming end: *Still alive.*

Yet life goes on, as we assume it will in the future, now with the living and later without them, us, me (1924–?).

12

The Romance of Ambition:
Memories of Saul Bellow

What it seems that I have taken up in my life, and continue to practice in the hope of improving my practice, is the vocation of literature. That's the evidence in the archeology of my past. At the end of the war my generation calls "our war," I knew where I needed to be.

Post–World War II Paris — ration cards, public baths if a person developed an interest in cleanliness, and a romance of ambition, the most reliable means of winter heating — took up its honored role once more for a hive of young American would-bees. Bruised and lovely, the paradise of misery was still the capital of hope.

Along with Richard Wright, the most esteemed American writer in residence during my years there, 1949–1951, was Saul Bellow, approximately ten years the senior of such as James Baldwin, Evan Connell, Terry Southern, Otto Friedrich, George Plimpton, Max Steele, and my callow self. Bellow had two published novels, *Dangling Man* and *The Victim*, appeared regularly in *Partisan Review*, collected a Guggenheim Fellowship. The rumor got around that he was destined to be America's new great novelist. His confident and graceful lounging, on view especially at the café Le Rouquet near Saint-Germain-des-Prés, seemed to confirm the rumor. He had a contract with the Viking Press. He was writing, and sometimes reading aloud, what would become *The Adventures of Augie March*. He was legal; the rest of us were stowaways.

We would-bees on our G.I. Bill money, our Fulbright money, our selling our clothes, cigarettes, and dollars on the black market, saw him as an Old Master in his early thirties. He had climbed the heights while some of us were still peddling hashish to gullible Frenchmen under the chic American name "marijuana," or serving as gigolos to existentialist millionaires, or worst of all, cadging handouts from family grinds back home. A few magazines, *Points, Janus, Zero*, and *DEATH* (the answer to Time Inc.'s *LIFE*), were started by young men and women of dependent means. We wouldn't get rich writing for Sindbad Vail's *Points*. Orson Welles gave the editor of *DEATH* a few bucks for food, which he shared with me in return for translating French restaurant menus; otherwise, he was reduced to ordering "Jumbo Omelet, goddammit! Omelet Jumbo!" which mysteriously always came with ham.

I watched Saul from across a terrace, at his ease, and tried to fit this boyish person to his book *The Victim*, about a New York summer hot as Bangkok and the mutual sufferings of a crazed anti-Semite and his prey, which I had read during my first summer back at school after the Army and the war. The dark-eyed young man with a shock of black hair and large-lipped smile was what a writer should look like. Also he wrote, I thought, as a writer should write, with acute sense, and an astringent alertness to events. Naturally, I didn't dare approach this formidable personage strolling under the plane trees or holding court in the cafés of the quarter.

I don't remember exactly how we met; perhaps he was amused by my lurking shy shadow. Without telling him, I sent the manuscript of my first novel, *Birth of a Hero*, to Viking, where it was dug out of the slush pile by a young editor, Monroe Engel, who shepherded it to higher authorities, including Malcolm Cowley. Since my return address was Paris, some prudent soul thought to ask Saul for an opinion — Had I really written the book? Would I be likely to repay investment by writing another book? — and he gave it a favorable verdict. Thanks partly to his generosity, I became a published novelist, returning to Cleveland, the Paris of Northeastern Ohio, after my Fulbright–G.I. Bill years in exile. I planned to buy a three-cent stamp at the post office in the Public Square, which would surely have my picture on it. (The novel came out, but it was still Benjamin Franklin on the three-cent stamp and Herb looking for work in a ham-and-eggs factory — whatever — to support self, wife, child, another child on the way.)

In Paris, with the news of imminent publication, I was adopted by some of the older expatriates, in addition to the French students, artists, and layabouts who had already become my Rive Gauche friends. Rodin's Balzac strutted belly-forward on his pedestal at Vavin-Montparnasse; encouraged by Sartre and de Beauvoir, huddling nearby at the Café de Flore and the Deux Magots, Diderot on his own pedestal pointed an accusing finger across the boulevard at the ancient church of Saint-Germain-des-Prés. Bellow was not a stony challenger; rather, an amiable deity for the fresh crop of

American would-bees seeking out the Paris of Henry Miller. Saul's generosity was not the sum of his appeal. His complaints, particularly marital, and his neediness, which went back to childhood or perhaps to the origins of the human species, gave him the charm of a genius for grief. His lamentations, which I thought of as "The Book of Saul," a long-run drama, had some of the eloquence of Job and Jeremiah; sackcloth, ashes, a wife who didn't understand him, and sometimes even worse, a woman who did. In that last variation, "The Book of Saul" departed scripture in the direction of modern happy endings.

When his marriage boiled over, the spillage was uncontained by the boundaries of family. The shock of seeing this hero in a state of frantic self-pity bewildered my twenty-two-year-old wife and my twenty-four-year-old self. He was a mature person, above the age of Jesus when crucified, but we were kids. With his first two books, his handsome lounging, and his renown as the Designated New Voice, his fall into despair made us feel awe. It was as if the mountain crumbled as we watched; we heard the shrieks.

Usually these family quarrels, hot tongue and cold shoulder, had to do with boredom (his) and jealousy (his wife's). He cultivated the admiration of pretty young women; he received it. He liked to recall how, when his first story was published in a national magazine, *Harper's Bazaar*, along with a photo, he received a telephone call from MGM Pictures. Did they want to make a movie of his story?

He beamed; high wattage. There was an ironic glint the large dark eyes. His smile delighted. No, they wanted to offer him a screen test.

When he glanced around the circle of admirers on the

terrace of Le Rouquet at the corner of the rue des Saints-
Pères and the boulevard Saint-Germain, we all responded
with an echo of his own joyous amusement, just as if we were
receiving the tale for the first time. Sometimes there was at
least one person present for whom it was new.

At the end of a sleety Paris winter, my wife Edith and I
thought of hitchhiking south for a while to pick figs and
swim in the Mediterranean. Saul had another dreadful long-
run battle in progress with Anita, his wife, and needed to get
away. He decided upon a strategic retreat to Spain by automobile, invited us to come along. We hoped to find cheap
digs in one of the French Basque towns near the Spanish border. This is how young we were; felt we were making a necessary political gesture by stopping short of visiting Franco's
Spain.

The trip in Saul's Citroën was no joyride. He wailed and
wept as we drove. He was also funny and full of curiosity
about himself and knew the map. I still connect his total recall for directions, his sensitive nose, with the quality of his
gift, an almost metabolic perspicacity. Through the narrow
medieval streets of Avignon, he found our way, sniffing out
the correct road. Ah, here would be a bread smell. And there
it was — a good bakery. There was also an unnerving claim
for attention to his marital agonies. His need was exclusive,
unflagging, draining. He required an audience as devoted as
the audience he gave himself.

Occasionally he rested from discourse about his conju-
gal griefs by talking about his book in progress, reading aloud
from *The Adventures of Augie March*. Although my approval

was a foregone conclusion, he asked for fresh and renewed bursts of enthusiasm. Occasionally, for a little variety, I tried to speak of my own novel-in-progress. But this really wasn't on the program.

In a park in Avignon, amid Roman ruins and blood-red meridional blooms, we saw a white-haired old man lovingly dandling a child. I said, "What a beautiful grandchild you have," and the man said, "My daughter." Perhaps I was fated not to satisfy my elders.

By the time we reached Banyuls, a few miles from the Spanish border, Edith and I were exhausted by the pleasure of Saul's company. Enough; we were stopping. The long afternoon on those narrow roads of the Côte de Vermeil, hearing of how only oblivion could offer Saul release from his sorrow, along with how his book would change the face of American literature, had left us hyperventilating. It was hot, bugs were swarming, and there may have been a mistral, that wind which makes folks crazier than usual.

We worried about leaving him alone in the hotel. We sat under an umbrella, drinking lukewarm soda, waving away the flies. We dreaded the meal we were about to have with him before we drove on into Spain. How would we cope with his paroxysms of despair?

She nudged my arm. "Look."

He was bounding toward us with a boyish grin, hair slicked down after his shower, eyes bright and skin fresh, chipper and restored. We were drained by the sufferings he seemed to shed. He was ready for a glass of wine and a good meal of the local fish stew, and his nose was twitching as he approved of the girls on their high wooden clogs in the town square of Banyuls-sur-Mer.

*   *   *

A few months later, with the eagerness of the would-be, I handed Saul a new story, "The Heart of the Artichoke." He was traveling to Italy and said he would take it with him. A week or so later I received the letter every young writer wishes to receive from a maestro (it even came from Rome, like an encyclical). In his clear and comely handwriting, it gave me clear and comely news I wanted. One odd phrase stood like a monument at the end of the paragraphs of perfect enthusiasm: "All barriers are down."

Through the inevitable discouragements to come, I remembered this grace note from on high and would mumble to myself, *All barriers are down . . . All barriers are down . . .* Surely all barriers must come down.

The zestful generosity of which the young Bellow was capable fills me with gratitude despite the narrower judgments of later years. It fits a time when birds sang sweetly in the courtyards of Paris and all our sleeves were stuffed with manuscripts.

In the early fifties, Saul's urban wit and angst — Kafka-out-of-Chicago, Dostoyevsky-from-the-yeshiva, polymathematical, polylinguistical, playful about it all — offered just the ticket for a G.I. Bill generation that was heading from college into graduate work, although its parents had often not finished high school. He made fun of suffering, he made the suffering into fun, he was fully implicated in his own life.

His personal grace relieved the solipsism. It wasn't that he didn't need others; he wooed those around him with an eloquent performance. He enacted his inner life for his public on the stage he carried everywhere. Women loved him; men found him demanding but ingratiating. He managed to enlist the world in the narrative of his disasters. Later, *Herzog*, drawn partly as an act of revenge after one of his marriage and friendship convulsions, would depict a beloved protagonist in a state of despair. Herzog ranted comically and proceeded from the melodramatic scenes with his wife to episodes with women eager to offer nursery solace. Such a scenario is unreal to experience — when mired in despair, most of us are not beloved — but Saul's star turn, dominating his own theater, helped to make it seem possible in his special case. Of course, talent and reputation contributed to what in the Kennedys came to be called charisma. He banged on his high chair with his spoon and asked to be served. He demanded respect and was in a position to get it. If he sometimes seemed like a child, he was a beautiful baby.

Saul's prose style married classical elegance to Mark Twain and the pungency of street speech; Yiddish played stickball with Henry James. As a young man, he rode the elements with terrific energy. He could spritz like a Lower East Side comedian and then lament like the prophets. His fate as a writer was to insist that words matter, his own most of all; suffering matters, his own absolutely; and he was able to enlist an audience in his struggle to survive, marked and measured by the works in progress that devoured his life.

He performed jazzy riffs on his good Hebrew-school, University of Wisconsin, and University of Chicago Trotskyite education, making neediness the baseline. ("I want, I want, I want.") He never questioned the appropriateness of his stance at the center of the stage. Among contemporary

novelists, he was surely the most serious about reading, studying, learning, and using it all, adding it all up. It was unified
by that keening cry from the heart. Saul needed, needed,
needed.

> Time . . .
> Worships language and forgives
> Everyone by whom it lives . . .

One morning in the late fifties, I drove, along with Ralph El-
lison and his big black dog, to Tivoli, New York, where
Ralph and Saul were sharing the rambling old Hudson River
house in which another of Saul's marriages ended. The dog
grew agitated from the long trip confined to an automobile,
and when Ralph stopped at an office at Bard College to pick
up his mail, the dog began furiously barking and leaping.
There seemed to be a discipline contest in progress between
Ralph and his dog. Ralph said, "Don't let him out," while
stately he proceeded to collect his mail.

Piteously disillusioned at this desertion by his master, the
dog let go a flood, a sheet, an avalanche of dog piss. I leapt
out of the car and the dog followed. Now the dog was zest-
fully leaping about on the green. My flanks were dripping.
Ralph reappeared, and commented with extreme irritation:

"I told you not to let him out."

Later, while I stood naked in the yard of the house,
hanging my soaked clothes on a line to dry, Saul talked about
the state of his career. "I want to be like Tolstoy," he said,
"more philosopher than anything else."

"More than a great novelist?" I asked, shivering, watching the steam rise from the clothes I had dipped into a soapy bucket.

"One more book," he said, "and my position will be impregnable."

In the house in Tivoli he read aloud from the manuscript of *Henderson the Rain King* while I tried to stifle my impatience, sometimes asking, "Couldn't I just read it by myself?" But he needed to hear his own voice, test his rhythms, bounce them off others. Since I was there, I would do.

In this novel I missed the gritty blues of his other books, his authentic monologuing plaint, and it seemed to me he was trying to put himself into a WASP aristocrat body, which he did not in fact possess. I wondered if he was competing with the New England writers he reacted against, while creating a fable indebted to Kafka and Melville. Was this part of constructing that "impregnable position"? I thought he was doing what he said not to do: writing from the head, not the heart — idea-writing, although in the end his heart's cry interrupted the plan.

As to building his reputation, *Henderson the Rain King* seems not to have been a mistake, even if the book had less appeal for some of his admirers. There are those who think it his best work. As he said of another writer's novels, it became a favorite for university instruction in American Lit courses. Professors enjoyed teaching it because there was so much to explain.

Himself, he didn't like to explain his writing, but he loved to read it aloud. "I'm a bird," he said, "not an ornithologist."

Until I came to live in San Francisco, our friendship went through ups and downs, with periods of intense intimacy;

that is, Saul confided his troubles, I listened and felt warm about being invited in. Occasionally he stayed with me in New York and gave me the difficult gratification of hinting that I stood between him and some desperate act at the high window. These threats didn't interfere with his intent sessions bent over the notebooks with their ruled lines upon which his fountain pen tracked his imagination and indignation. I learned that folks don't usually kill themselves in the middle of composing the suicide note.

I sought his approval for my own writing and sometimes got it. His words were used in advertising my books. I was still a young writer; he was a maestro; I was both grateful and privileged to share his life's disasters.

When I left the East Coast, thereby becoming unavailable during crises, the ups and downs or our friendship transformed themselves into a prolonged down. We exchanged letters for a while, but he needed regular nursing care. Others filled the requirement. I was irritated that he didn't include "The Heart of the Artichoke," a story that he had praised so highly, in an anthology he edited. "I forgot," he said, shrugging. "Why take such a thing seriously? I just forgot."

He was right. It was merely my own writer's vanity that was aggrieved, but the advice not to take it seriously was hard to accept, coming from a writer whose spirit could be broken by a slighting review in the *Deseret News*.

In the early sixties, as a member of the international jury meeting in various European locales to award the Formentor Prize, I argued for Saul Bellow to receive the award. One year the favored French candidate was Nathalie Sarraute, a leader of the fashionable *nouveau roman* grouplet. As a friend of her daughter, I had known her during my student days in Paris.

(The daughter's husband pro tem was the journalist Stanley Karnow. He and I bought little Renault 4CV automobiles at the same time, and our wives had in common resentment of our rude habit of running outdoors when it rained, sometimes raining on them in our leaky rooms, to make sure our cars were not melting. Stan and I were enjoying the simultaneous strains of first wives and first vehicle ownership.)

The Formentor deliberations were supposed to be secret; they were, of course, not, especially since the French delegation did not get its way about Nathalie Sarraute. Saul Bellow received the prize.

Later, when I saw Nathalie Sarraute in Paris, the grand old lady looked me keenly in the eye and greeted me with a mantra that she repeated fairly frequently that Paris season: "*Ah, 'Airbair'! C'est vous le gangster.*"

Barney Rosset of Grove Press, organizer of the American delegation, asked me to present the award at a ceremony in New York. I felt pleased to have made a case, pleased for Saul, although at that point in our long friendship, we were not close. We were not really friends anymore. But as always when I saw him, the old warmth and gratitude welled up.

I handed him the check. Photographs were taken for the newspapers. We ate canapés, drank wine. A woman showed up who had been a lover of Saul's, then found employment as a character in one of his books, and she picked an argument with me. "The really great writer, the one who should have been given the prize" — the writer she was currently studying — "is Ionesco. He's international."

"I like his plays." I said. "*The Lesson, The Bald Soprano*, they've been running forever at the Théâtre de la Huchette. When I'm in Paris and I see the posters, I know nothing has changed around there, no matter that everything has changed."

"*Rhinoceros!*" she cried. "The metaphors, the mythos! Compared to Ionesco, Saul is only . . ." She wouldn't say it. She shook her curls with that ferocity that he captured in his fictional portrayal. "And take it from me, I know," she announced, mandibles compressed, teeth gritting.

I remembered his image of a woman hiding a dagger in her stocking.

"Saul was, let me tell you how that bozo treated me — compared to Ionesco —"

Maybe it was in her garter belt, that dagger.

Herzog turned out to be Saul's most popular book, his best selling novel after *The Adventures of Augie March*, which had first broken through for a large public. Comic and sad, spiced with rants in the form of letters, Herzog was drawn directly from his personal travails, cuckoldry, a turbulent divorce, treason by a protégé. He put the wife, the protégé, and friends into the book with hardly any disguise, as if the story was intended not so much to be about them as against them. The letters Herzog wrote to world figures were entertaining, garrulous, alternately wise, crazed, and self-mocking. He poured himself into the man-with-heart, Herzog, ranting, wronged, the seeker betrayed.

Self-justification gave an aspect of troubling ambiguity to the book. He intended to be the American Dostoyevsky, but funny; the American Tolstoy, but a close witness to the times. But neither of his Russian masters would have portrayed himself as innocently aggrieved and yet fatally attractive to women. Most men know from experience that, when overwhelmed by jealousy, they are in a mood to grovel, whine, and smell bad — not very attractive to women. They may find nurses, but the sexy and delightful women tend to cross the road when they slump into view.

Herzog, despite his frenzies, remains the most charming man in the world; or so Saul seemed to hope; or so he wrote him. This made his revenge on life too perfect. The novel was flawed by its special pleading, its lyric of self-love.

Perhaps what made me uneasy appealed to both the public at large and the Nobel committee. Herzog's dire suffering didn't get in the way of fun. The letters to the great, alive and dead, were elegant paranoid monologues, marinated in Saul's learning and his moral passion to change the world, or at least punish it. The challenges of disaster in love and friendship, divorce laws and night sweats, were given chipper colors and a style that reached for the lugubrious in a middle-aged scholar's yearning. Bathroom spying approached French farce mechanism, with no French farce mechanism cool. Yet the book allows readers to perch on the benches as spectators at a circus of pain. It didn't disturb too much. The trapeze whirled, and the clown fell safely into the sawdust. The elephants danced, dropped their elephant doo on the fallen clown, and he arose as a hero, covered with flowers, embraced by all. The book was an original and intelligent entertainment, a consolation.

A mutual friend of ours, call him Professor X, wrote to Saul to congratulate him on his Nobel Prize and also to give his response to *Herzog*. Professor X, a man with severe and incurable physical problems, in lifelong pain, wrote admiringly of the book and with delight about the acclaim from Sweden, but added a fateful sentence: "Of course, your novel doesn't solve my problems."

Saul cut off all connection. Professor X was bewildered and hurt. He was about to retire from his job; his body was rapidly giving way. I hoped to be an intermediary, described the troubles of our friend, and asked Saul why he was so angry. "I can't be interested in what goes on with him," he said.

"What happened?"

"He wrote me a poison-pen letter."

The author of *Herzog*, with a protagonist who poured his advice, suggestions, and complaints into the mails, had received a letter from an old friend, which ended a long association. This seemed a bizarre twist on the novel. I believe the letter must have been ruder than Professor X had said. I asked to see a copy, and of course like a good academic, Professor X had made one. The letter was dense with praise and goodwill. But it did contain that offense: *your novel doesn't solve my problems . . .*

All the honors available worldwide couldn't relieve Saul's touchiness. Receiving hundreds of clippings with rave notices, he was still the man who could be thrown into a raging funk by that bad review in the *Deseret News* of Salt Lake City (it may have been the *Rocky Mountain News* of Denver, Colorado).

Among the later books, *Humboldt's Gift* — not a favorite of many critics — stood out for me as a comic and terrified riff on desperation and madness. It was intended partly as a tribute to Saul's friend and contemporary, the poet Delmore Schwartz, who in his paranoia turned against Saul as he turned against almost everyone. Saul tried to help him, contributed money for treatment, but could not escape the wrath of a man spinning out of control. Schwartz died miserable and alone in a seedy Manhattan hotel.

The book celebrated the charm of a manic talent; it also memorialized the friendship of Bellow and Schwartz, contemporaries and buddies. The engrossing persuasiveness of Schwartz, the ranting and pathos, were named; and the book expressed the helplessness of those around him. What Saul couldn't do was to evoke the great gifts of Delmore Schwartz, the brilliance of his best writing, the loopy wit and the elegiac mourning. He named the madman; he couldn't name the perverse genius.

This is a most daunting task for a novelist, to suggest genius in one of his characters. But it also seemed that Saul couldn't really allow the competition from his friend, and instead needed to hold him up for regard as a pathetic specimen, a loser.

Out of the quarrel with ourselves, Yeats said, we make poetry; and out of the quarrel with others we make war. In his novels, Saul made both poetry and his own kind of war, which could have resulted in mere vengeful tale-telling. At his best, he managed to transmute his antagonists, wives, lovers, and failed friends into grand sports and aberrations. Early on, he preserved in this circus world the sense of himself as a tragic clown, dancing amid the wreckage. Later, he seemed to feel that this image was beneath his dignity, and as his books became more severe, they lost some of their grace. *Mr. Sammler's Planet*, tense and controlled, was a parable of withdrawal, rejection of a world that lets us down. Through the optic of the aging survivor, Sammler, he makes a case for depression as the proper response to the disaster of modern history.

Still later, the wintry authenticity of *The Dean's December* is a confession of hopeless yearning. Flashes of the old comedy raise ironic signposts as the writer charts a continuing devolution into disappointment.

In the early seventies I found myself in Chicago with the woman who had become my second wife. I loved her, I was proud of her — called her the "statistical miracle" because it seemed such extraordinary good luck to find her — and I wanted Saul to appreciate my good fortune, too. He invited us to lunch at the club where he played racquetball. It was elegant and sparkly, with a panoramic view of the city, Saul's city.

The three of us had a polite and affable meal; fish, a good wine. In my pride I waited impatiently for a word alone with him. At last she stood up to go to the bathroom, and I watched him as he watched her. The he turned to me with his wide smile and said, "She has a sense of humor. I like that in a woman."

I was chagrined. I wanted him to express enthusiasm for my statistical miracle; this smug and bland okay was surely not enough. But it was all he had to give me just then. My joy was no pleasure to him during another crisis in his life. I was no longer one of his intimates.

Melissa returned to the table and my heart leapt with love and pride, and Saul's opinion didn't matter.

I was no longer an acolyte or disciple. The ten-year difference in our ages was becoming irrelevant as the years rolled by. Saul mattered, but not enough to spoil my time with the woman I loved. And also not enough to make me read his novels without judgment. The supple prose was engrossing; how he danced with ideas! Sometimes I didn't like the vision behind the prose.

At various times he championed the work of younger writers like Edward Hoagland, William Kennedy, and Cormac McCarthy, and he was often moving and generous in praise of suffering contemporaries like Isaac Rosenfeld, Delmore Schwartz, John Berryman, and John Cheever, especially after they died. He acutely felt the loss of his contemporaries, those who fought to stay afloat and failed at it, as he had fought and succeeded.

When he turned against old friends, such as a lawyer in Chicago whom he lampooned in one book, he was merciless, and they felt crushed. I know three people who wrote novels intended as revenge for what he had written about them (the books were not published; rage and frustration provided unreliable fuel for inspiration). When Saul wrote a book against, he had larger things in mind than self-justification and punishment of enemies. Freshets of soul and wit scampered through the prose, as if his essence were a glacier, the top warmed by the sun, chunks breaking off and sparkling streams pounding down the ice.

When asked at a lecture to explain something about one of his books, boyish irritation, that winsome flirtiness he could summon, arose in his voice as he grinned, seemed to search, rediscovered his mantra for a new audience: "I'm a bird, not an ornithologist." Once again he was saying it for the first time. He threw back his head in laughter, encouraged others to relax and laugh, and even the questioner joined in.

In the fall of 1988 or 1989, I heard he was depressed

about the breakup of another marriage, the death of a brother and a childhood friend, and telephoned him. We had a few meals together; I attended a lecture he gave at NYU. At first, as we caught up with his life, there was a warmth that recalled our old friendship. The morning he left Manhattan, he invited me to meet him for breakfast at One Fifth Avenue, so I was surprised to feel over the toast and eggs that I was imposing on him. He was withdrawn and chilly. Had I said the wrong thing about his lecture? Had I offended him again by mentioning Jack Ludwig?

The son who accompanied him seemed embarrassed by his father and made a point of being cordial to me. When we said good-bye, Saul stood there, nattily dressed as usual, in a stylish coat and hat like an international businessman, waiting stiffly apart from us as his son and I chatted. Finally he said impatiently, "Come on, we're going," and that was good-bye.

I had written him no poison-pen letters, but somehow I fell into the category of those who offended. I tried to imagine how this happened — by growing up, by insufficient discipleship, by not being available to listen to his troubles since I lived in California, by admiring other writers besides him (he was annoyed by my enthusiasm for Vladimir Nabokov), by no reason that was clear to me. Like so many former friends, I was out of the privileged circle.

Some of the friends he did keep played variations on the theme of disciplehood. One woman liked to say she only lived in Chicago "so I can be there for Saul." As she murmured "Saul used to read his new pages to me every day," or "When Saul's upset, I always tell him . . . ," or the ever-popular "Sometimes when Saul can't sleep, I . . . ," people formed the natural habit of asking if she was having an affair with him. It was a question urged upon them; rude not to ask. Primly she would fall silent, a silence that cried *Yes! Yes!* But having been urged toward the question, folks felt general relief that she was discreet enough not to admit to the affair she very likely hadn't had.

More than fifty years of friendship and non-friendship include too many harsh memories. They begin, after gratitude, with that ordinary puzzlement that a writer and a man who inspired part of a generation, altered the tone of a literary period, wrote with such grace, nonetheless lived his life with flaws both large and petty, like other people. The flaws seemed to be magnified by the fineness of his achievement. Saul wrote in the rhythms of city speech, stylized, pursuing the sense of his troubled American life. His anxiety made him frantic. He reflected upon each moment, defending himself with wit and charm. Again and again, he almost, temporarily, mastered his experience. And then the victory passed. He draped his life's story in a prose that served to calm him — almost, temporarily — by displaying his nakedness fetchingly clothed. The narrative sometimes had the innocence of a boyish daydream, sometimes of a boy's nightmare. The discourse both quickened and heartened his readers.

And it wasn't just style, the playful surface, the watchfulness. He really wanted to discover What It All Meant (he would never put it that way). His gifts enabled him to edge abruptly into scenes of vivid desire and grief, as in the last paragraphs of the great story, *Seize the Day*. During his best moments, he shared his sense of our lives in a way impossible for writers of mere self-justification and confession. The path of self-justification, he used to say, has been worn so deep that all you can see is the top of the heads of the writers who follow it.

The images in *The Victim* of a pair of tormentors chained together one hot summer in New York, or Augie March wrestling with Chicago, or Humboldt raving in the grip of mania, and especially Tommy Wilhelm, the protagonist of *Seize the Day*, weeping for himself and mankind at the funeral of someone he doesn't know, will endure as the memories of Saul's personal faults fade. Tolstoy, Dostoyevsky, Melville, Kafka, D. H. Lawrence, and Unamuno were not saints in real life, either. Their work and Saul's teach something about generosity.

The effect of his presence was also generous for other writers. The example of his success invited to the feast those who followed after him in the priestly — rabbinic! — calling of storyteller, lyric poet, questing philosopher. For a later generation, his rich use of vernacular speech energized the American language as Rabelais and Verlaine did for French, as Shakespeare and Laurence Sterne did in English, as Whitman and Mark Twain did. Of this doing and redoing, there needs to be no end. The stylistic playfulness, grace, and grasp of American urban yearning by a writer from a Yiddish-speaking family resonated especially for other Jews. We, too, could be Americans in the American language. I am old enough to have been informed by a friendly editor that I should spell my name "Gould" when a first story of mine appeared in her magazine. Later, a writer who had changed his name to something bland and generic informed me, with a grin both stern and smug, that he could be a real American writer, but I, alas, burdened by the name "Gould," could not. After Saul's success, writers who once believed they needed names like "Shaw," "Harris," or "Algren" no longer required these "Made in America" labels. They could call themselves Ginsberg, Litwak, Leavitt, Canin, Gold, whatever names they came with, and this was liberating.

Saul's persistent heartfelt *I want, I want, I want* — his own cry and that of his protagonists — really means *I need, I need, I need*. Insatiability derived both from his condition as an outsider and increasing recognition that being inside is no solution, either. Sometimes he glamorized his neediness by turning it into heroic appetite, as in *Henderson the Rain King*, elegantly, but with a querulous edge, in a bewildering rush of haughty self-pity. No story or novel could settle matters for him. He never stopped trying. He turned away congratulations for his many prizes (Nobel, Pulitzer, National Book Award) by confiding that they interfered with his real business.

He wanted to be like Tolstoy, both a teller of tales and an inspirer, a moral philosopher; and he wanted to solve his own problems. He kept on trying, sustained by the devotion of Janis, his fifth wife. He became something like a shadow Tolstoy, running toward a devoted woman instead of away from her. An older Tolstoy wrote his passionate novella *Hadji Murad*, hot-eyed and rampaging over terrain he knew from his youth, after the great periods of *War and Peace*, *Anna Karenina*, and *The Death of Ivan Ilyich*. Then, overwhelmed, he turned to the autumnal achievements of *The Kreutzer Sonata*, "What Is Art?" and the fabular tracts with which he sought to teach moral lessons while his own family life fell into ruins. The spare precision of Bellow's first novels, *Dangling Man* and *The Victim*, opened into the rich language-busting of *The Adventures of Augie March*. Swaggering and full of delight at rafting down the wide river of American speech, he broke patterns as Twain and Whitman had, giving the street and the library equal place. And then, avidity still the habit he lived by, he became less hungry. He judged the century and found it lacking. The rebellious dangling man, the Trotskyite who had studied the violin and anthropology, became a defender of the established order, frightened by rock music and the Chicago he helped redefine. It made me fear my own old age to look into those great dark eyes and see the laughter in retreat.

Strolling with Saul down the rue de Verneuil during the early days of our friendship, around the rue du Bac, back up to the café Le Rouquet — across the street from the garden of the Russian church — talking and talking amid that particular Paris smell of Gauloise Bleu, red-wine piss, and flowers, I happened to speak of Sinclair Lewis, who was still alive and writing his worn-out, alcoholic last novels. As a boy, when I first discovered grownup books, *Babbitt*, *Main Street*, and *It Can't Happen Here* opened doors to the world outside Lakewood, Ohio. But by 1950 it seemed that Sinclair Lewis's fingers were merely punching the type-writer, his rage had devolved to hysteria, the satire was diminished into abuse of a world he no longer fathomed. Sinclair Lewis's erotic yearning — I was in my early twenties — seemed pathetic in an old man.

Saul interrupted, turning his warm and amused gaze on me, with a reproach that was aimed exactly right. "Don't count any writer out while he's still alive," he said.

These words imposed a long silence. I had a vision of eternity like the one called forth by Oscar J. Campbell, when our class read Lucretius on time and death, and he spoke of his stroke and then stopped speaking, lowering his head in contemplation of the unknowable. I accepted the shame Saul's reminder brought down upon me.

Through difficult times in a long friendship, the early paradox remains, young Saul in crisis, that smiling person with rosy cheeks and hair freshly wetted by his shower, bouncing down mossy steps toward the café in Banyuls where we waited for him more than a half century ago. Edith and I expected someone exhausted by griefs without end on the roads from Paris to the Côte de Vermeil. Instead, what appeared for the bouillabaisse and wine was an avid young winner, sure of his powers. We had been exhausted by listening to his suffering. He was refreshed by the telling of it.

The irritable old person in gray and black who warily and impatiently pulled away from our encounter in New York still lived by the standard of that passionate and spend-thrift willfulness. Since he was an artist, still alive, still alive, he couldn't be counted out. Within his irritability still swelled the indomitable young writer with pains he adored, restlessly seeking how to say them better.

Among my brother Sid's papers after his death, I found a letter from Saul to me, written in the early sixties, in response to a story of Sid's that I had sent to *The Noble Savage*, the journal Saul edited. Saul's letter was full of good counsels and generous encouragement, and I gave it to my brother in the hope that it would nudge him toward finishing the endless, never completed novel he spent a lifetime writing.

I wrote Saul in a flood of remembrance and gratitude and in sadness for our faded friendship. His reply was immediate and full of compassion about losses, his own and mine, of my brother, and regret that we had "neglected to attend to our friendship."

We were back in touch, attending to friendship. He wrote tenderly about Janis, his last wife, who kept him alive, he said, through caring, love, and the example of her youth. When he was eighty-four and she was pregnant, some women expressed anger at what they considered sexist behavior. There is no symmetry in the matter; a man of eighty-four can father a child. "I try to keep in practice," he said. Justice is hardly the point here.

On a balmy day in October 1999, we had lunch outdoors at the Nob Hill Café in San Francisco, and then sat in the sun on a bench in Huntington Park, both of us — I'm not reading minds here — remembering our Paris days when we used to pass the time like this. But we weren't talking about Sartre, Merleau-Ponty, or the daily news of the trials of Nazi collaborators. He talked about his life in Boston and Vermont, about his regret for needing to fly with a helper now that his wife's pregnancy was too advanced for her to travel with him. She wanted their child. She knew what the conditions were. He spoke of his end of the deal with a certain wryness, with an energetic resignation, his head cocked as he laughed about oncoming inevitabilities. "I always prided myself on my sense of smell. I always prided myself on my memory. I'm losing them." When he laughed, throwing his head back, he was a boy again.

And then he said it was time for his nap. He took my arm as we walked back to the Huntington Hotel. That night he was having dinner with his eldest son, Gregory, whom I had known as a child in Paris. "He has gripes about me he doesn't want to give up," he said. "I don't blame him." But this father, grandfather, and father-to-be intended to mend his fences at a crucial time.

For me, Saul is still fully present. There was a generous dreamer locked within his vanity, a young poet and lover in the body of the wary old party; and when he emitted his voice, sent out his courting signals to the world, which he desperately asked to understand him — often in scenes filled with pleading and tears — he managed to bring something gallant into our lives. He helped to create a new permission, not only for Jewish writers, but also for others previously ex-iled to an odd regionality without regions — blacks, Latinos, second- and third-generation immigrants, founding sons of not-founding fathers. Like all artists, his personality was stuffed with surprises, and not always delightful ones; like all human beings.

When the days and nights end for a writer, something keeps going on if he has shed his magic light and darkness upon the miracle of life. "The death of the poet is kept from the poems." And Saul Bellow struggled to leave us a record of days and nights that would not disappear after his troubled and fortunate time on earth.

Afterword

These pages are about love and memory, about why both are blessings and sorrows and a form of immortality. There's some repetition, or, as I prefer to define it, elaboration. (Complaints may be addressed to the Literary Structure Licensing Bureau.) This is a book about aging and time passing, and also about time moving forward into the uncharted future; about aging and time passing, and about not aging and time standing still. The L. S. Licensing Bureau is open for business all day, all night.

Provisionally Facing Facts (In an Interim Sort of Way)

> These our actors,
> As I foretold you, were all spirits and
> Are melted into air, into thin air. . . .

Francis Xavier, Victor, Beatrice's avidly loyal husband Harold . . . I hope their last breath will be peaceful despite the uncanny rattle of matters closing down. They struggle to conceal their future by reclaiming the past, remaking it in their dreams. If I squint at myself, I can see me doing the same, as if there were no last rattle of breath in my program.

In the sexual ramble, the human creature differs from more sensible beasts. We dream of completion by joining another. Many of us are never too old to be juvenile, just as we're never too young to be emptied, worn-out. A randy old guy like Yeats, years-laden, pursued his longing, by means of his avid last lyrics in avid grasping toward a lovely young woman. The old man on a stick still danced, had to, thought he could. "When the mouth dies, what is there?"

"Who speaks of love has sad eyes," sang Jean Ferrat. He who dreams of love has sad eyes, usually. Those who need love to save them often have sad eyes. Old men and old women have sad eyes. It's called "experience." Sometimes, for the fortunate ones, the tired eyes are wrinkled with merriment.

Lovers, when in love, have happy eyes.

There used to be carnival midways, there still are a few, but if they disappear entirely, our lives on earth will still be turbulent and filled with delight and deceit, like a carnival midway. If there were a God, his all-seeing eyes would have to be tearless as He observes us from afar. His tears would run out; too exhausting even for a God to observe our actions without smiling during our brief span between the endless past and the future. Surely, while laughing, He would squeeze out one more tear. Older than Francis Xavier, Victor, Howard, but perhaps still a lover in his own fashion, He should also have sad eyes.

There were years I expended in philosophical self-questioning, trying to deal with a dilemma. Did I want a woman of intellect, kindness, and an instinct for good times, or a woman with an irresistible leg (preferably two), shining hair, and the etcetera of physical bounty nature endowed her with? Many late dinners ensued as a product of this dubious quest. I didn't resolve the question as I should have. Instead, I decided: Both! I want both, I need both! I'll find a reader of Kierkegaard who rocks, a woman with sly glances after that late dinner whose eyes also brim with feeling when we listen together to the Mozart *Requiem*. I was corrupted by personal ads before I ever read one. Optimistic American trial and error led to a harvest of five children.

Although not a medical expert or biotech researcher like so many in northern California, I've identified my disease as Restless Beatnik Syndrome with Nosy Metaphysical Complications. My doctor doesn't have a remedy, so I've self-medicated with Mozart, Bob Dylan, Woods-Walking, and Café-Sitting. This chronic condition hasn't worn off during the twenty-first century. Earlier, I joined my fellow postwar young would-bees who booked third-class passage to France in search of Henry Miller, Ernest Hemingway, horse meat and cheap Algerian wine in a time of no heat, food rationing, bad teeth, and the massive intention of Paris to become Paris again, the capital of hope and the paradise of misery; absolutely not Lakewood, Ohio, or Stockton, California, or even Brooklyn, New York. We had the G.I. Bill, we had Fulbrights; some had trust funds or family happy to get rid of them; we had clothes, cigarettes, or bodies to sell; we had black market hustles. We would be young forever, and forever friends and rivals, both in the making of Art, Truth, & Beauty and the selling of hashish to French existentialists under the chic Marshall Plan label of "Le Marijuana Américain." (It wasn't at all. It was mere Algerian hemp, the gullible existentialists thereby financing our purchase of an equally rancid product, Algerian wine.)

We were multitaskers, due to financial and hormonal imperatives, needing money for heat, coffee, black market food, and lessons in French from lovely, sallow, bad-teethed French girls called Juliette or Chérie. Mason Hoffenberg and Terry Southern found time to write *Candy* between café deliveries of *le marijuana Américain*. We also had the task of hanging out, measuring the literary competition, including Saul Bellow and Harry Hershkowitz (who?). I had an additional problem, a wife married after three years in the U.S. Army, which had trained me in weaponry, parachuting, and the Russian language, but had neglected to prepare me for her.

When a rosy-cheeked young man, Otto Friedrich, scored an interview with André Gide ("Gide liked me and I liked him") and then George Santayana in Rome ("Santayana liked me and I liked him"), we tried to overcome our jealousy by saying this was mere journalism. (Although I liked journalism and wanted journalism to like me.) Otto later wrote good books about Germany and Hollywood, edited *The Saturday Evening Post*, hired me to interview Vladimir Nabokov.

We thrived in the yellow-gray Paris light. At the predawn hours, I sometimes left my room at the Hôtel de Verneuil, which also housed Jimmy Baldwin, an androgynous Norwegian journalist, a film buff who changed his name to Stein in honor of Gertrude Stein, a Dutch painter whom a little bug-eyed Spaniard tried to visit, plus — *hélas!* — the first wife I had married for poor reasons. When I politely asked the Spanish visitor to the hotel, the one with the hyperthyroid eyes, how to identify him for the Dutch painter, he pronounced his name clearly: "*Mais c'est moi, Pi-cas-so.*"

It was a crowded world of heavy smoking and bathneeding international Francophiles at the hotel aslant on its rotten timbers. A lover of night and silence, an aficionado of time away from the wife married by mistake, I walked before dawn to Vavin-Montparnasse to commune with the Rodin statue of Balzac on its pedestal near the Dôme café, not far from the Select. The cafés were shut at this hour, wicker chairs chained to the terraces, and even the transvestite club, Le Jockey, had discharged its last sad group of clothes-wearers. I stood in front of Balzac in the iron cloak, which seemed to make his belly even more naked, forward, and arrogant, and I vowed like Rastignac at the world: *It's between us two now!* It was a contest between one buzzing would-be against the other would-bees to conquer our yearnings by fulfilling them. At that age, I never considered this might be a permanent state of contention.

In later life, sometimes called "late life," "those golden sunset years," and treated as a person in that state by courteous younguns on San Francisco buses when they leap up to offer a seat to Chinese ladies laden with pink plastic shopping bags or gray-bearded writers, I found for myself a third alternative to the two categories of the True Love variety pak. Perhaps some are intended to live alone. The facts on the ground and the feet in my shoes have spread. I've learned something new, although I still move in hiking boots, don't shuffle in slippers. Behind the wheel at a stoplight, I might yet catch the eye of a Kierkegaard fan in a white tennis dress, and transform into Francis Xavier, Victor, or Harold. I don't have far to go. Man's fate is provisional until his spirit is melted into air, into thin air.

> I'll be a better person, a better man,
> Really do it, if I can

Persistence and the Green Fuse

When applying language to life as a way of living it, I prefer the word "oldguy," even if it isn't a word, to the words "sliding downhill," "senile," or "gaga" (French pejorative). I don't wear a bus pass strung on a shoelace around my neck. No one has yet offered to help me find my way home from the corner store. I'm cheerful in the morning, which experience tells me can displease overnight residents or visitors.

Lack of a natural gift for melancholy is a disturbance, taken as a failure of human fret. However, life has made up for the flaw by giving me instructions in desolation, a lesson I didn't choose. The morning when a telephone call awakened me with news of a helicopter accident is forever lodged in every day. Sleepless predawn alertness brings the news; rain brings the news, so does the sunrise; the eyes of my children remind me, although nowadays we seldom speak of the event. Melissa, the mother of our sons and daughter, died a few days before her forty-eighth birthday. When they do speak of it, our sons and daughter say she didn't die, she was killed, because her life ended when she was still captivatingly, enchantingly vigorous and young. She and I had scheduled a birthday lunch together. I had propped a birthday gift for her at my door, not that I'd forget. Now I forget what I did with it.

I telephoned our children, one by one, first saying "Please sit down," and listened to the empty moment followed by breathlessness and choking; and then called her parents and heard her mother cry, "But she was our star!" and then her always cheerful, matter-of-fact, graciously controlled father shrieking. And then I called my other daughters. And then I tried to set about making arrangements. An official first said I should come to identify the body and then, apologetically, telephoned to say this would not be necessary. So I continued making arrangements.

Melissa and I lost each other to divorce. We lost each other in her death. I've never lost the history that we loved each other. She took my arm like a happy lover when we were happy lovers. Separation didn't stop the continual flow. The urgent unlost past endures, like all history; good and bad, it endures, persists, simply continues, like all that once marked the world. The vibration of the butterfly's wings over her wicker picnic basket on a sun-drenched slope of Mount Tamalpais may seem to have vanished after its brief stay with us, but the universe is changed by it, by the crab sandwiches, by the thermos of wine. When Ari grins, when Ethan casts his sideways challenging glance at me, when Nina gazes into the eyes of her baby, Melissa's grandchild, my grandchild, I see in them the restless enchantress whose wide blue gaze was as thrilling as the butterfly's brief fluttering over our first lunch on a mountainside meadow with the Pacific Ocean also glowing blue and restless below. "Why does the grass stand straight up to reach for the sun, but we're just lying here with our toes dangling?" she asked, laughing. I think I murmured, "Heliotropic," which of course was a phenomenon she knew very well, and she tapped my mouth with a finger. When she turned her attention to me or anyone, she had that magic gift of making the recipient of her attention the center of the universe. Even if he was not. But he could think he was.

Something this woman was in herself, a steady willfulness within her restlessness, an intention to please but no regret if she didn't, an open heart and a guarded soul, may have been as much an enigma to her as it was to others. She was available to what might come next. She waited for adventure to happen to her, expecting everything or nothing good, ready to move on as always, as she knew she could, to another career, another husband, another everything or nothing. Surely whatever came next would be better, as the not yet experienced adventure always surely will be.

I wrapped my arms and legs around her. She was more than a handful. She was more than arms, legs, or my praise, "a statistical miracle," could hold, but when I joined my body with hers and she clasped me close, I knew I was in possession of the universe.

Then in the evening when she announced that life was too complicated, she had to divorce someone, she couldn't divorce our three children, it wouldn't be fair — it had to be me. She revealed that she had felt deserted when I flew to Africa to report on the Biafran civil war in Nigeria. "You didn't tell me!" I said. "You were supposed to know," she answered, and added the proof: "I was a mother with a six-month-old baby."

Complete in herself, and also she hid that she was not complete in herself. Lovers may think they hide nothing, but they hide. Their arms wrapped around each other brings a completeness of two together that seems to validate and redeem everything lost and failed in the past. Embracing, they forget for a time the griefs that precede these moments and, inevitably, follow them.

Everything that lovers have ever had seemed to me to be ours. Who on earth deserves such a blessing? No one, but I accepted it anyway. This couldn't be, yet it was, then it wasn't, and finally it forever is, like the butterfly's flutter. Others have also flown close to the sun and then fallen to earth, a place populated by perished love.

Melissa died in a storm in a helicopter, along with her new husband-to-be. It's proper that our children don't use the word "died." They believe it was not in her nature to die. They correct me. She was *killed*.

Let's not die before we get old, as a song suggests; instead, follow the advice of another song Ethan chose to be played at his mother's funeral, the cranky voice of Bob Dylan reminding her friends, family, and former husband that it is preferable to have one more cup of coffee before we go. One more, even if that intention defies nature, one more.

Until the death rattle vibrates in my chest, the program is to get on with living. On a hot October evening in San Francisco, winds just right, no fog, the sky glowing purplish with reflections off America's great metropolitan village, streetlamps and starlight, I climb Russian Hill after a dinner alone. There's an unaccustomed sweat stain on my shirt when I peel it off. It looks like a cumulus cloud. I wonder if it predicts a coming cardiac storm. My pulse is steady, but I feel the pressure from the climb in my legs. I slump into a chair, taking a telephone call from Ann, my eldest daughter, asking, "Are you okay, Dad? You didn't call me today."

"No stroke, no heart attack, dear daughter. Fine, fine, fine."

Then I stand to go brush my teeth and I'm steady on my feet. That's my opinion and I'm sticking with it.

Perhaps a person can be genetically engineered to be

hopeful by an arrangement of chromosomes just next door to the genes or chromosomes for psychopathy, the character disorder of uncaring people. Without doing the lab work, in anecdotal self-defense: I read newspapers with concern, I've suffered loss and defeat, and understand that even a federal judgeship would only be a lifetime appointment. The end is in store. So: fine, fine, fine.

Death is the reward we all get for living. Rich and poor, bad, good, and the merely okay, everyone gets it in the end. Almost everyone is sometimes turbulent with zest, sometimes becalmed, stagnant, morose. Those who bullied themselves, sulked and groped through their lives, oppressed those who were weak or needy . . . Finally all of us together experience this mysterious darkness, this blankness. We drink of the glass what we can as thirsty human creatures. It's both half full and half empty.

Chagall dances with his fiddle on the rooftop; Yeats prances around on his old man's stick. Francis Xavier, Victor, and Howard from my hometown of Cleveland also do their best to preserve their charmed moments. I would forgive their foolishness, if only I wanted to. I should. I realize the glow in the windless San Francisco sky, that rich fading purple, which so pleased me, urging me to speed up Russian Hill, bringing the cloud of sweat to my shirt, was partly the reflection of light off the city and partly the result of auto exhaust, lung-eating smog.

The Encroaching Inevitable

Sometimes it's time to excavate the accumulation of a life in the flat I've rented for forty-eight years (temporarily, I explain to visitors). My son suggests that I hire storage space for the debris, but if I did, wouldn't I lose track of relics that emerge and emerge anew like the rocks on the terraced mountain slopes of Haiti, where peasants clear, farm, clear again? Recently I found a Photomaton strip, one of those four-for-a-dollar relics, from the time when the thrill was to press into a booth with a girlfriend, mugging for the apparatus and, incidentally, rubbing against each other for the sake of rubbing against each other. Nobody's fault; it's crowded in there. That girlfriend of long ago is now a shadow of the past, but so am I — that grinning beatnik with a freshly grown beard and much untrimmed hair.

My hairs are, today, still frequently untrimmed. The beard is short, with white bristles. My children are engaged in a campaign to make me less of a 1950s beatnik, although they have other and more fruitful careers to pursue. "Dad, you can afford bookcases — why the planks and boxes?"

"I like them."

"A rug that wouldn't show the lining wouldn't hurt, Dad."

"This one's okay. I got it at Cost Plus during the Blizzard of Ought Eleven."

"And what if there's another earthquake, Dad" — reminding me that the self-portrait given me by Zero Mostel fell in the earthquake of 1989, the glass shattering.

"If something falls, it'll probably fall on the rug lining, not me. So far, that's how it seems to work out. I haven't been killed even once."

Ignoring protests, Ari bought bookcases and fit them in while I stood by, trying to uncross my arms (Cleveland defiance) and go with the flow (California grooviness). Nina brought me a new rug and pointed out the advantages of surviving uncrippled when walking barefoot. My toes won't catch in accumulated holes. Ethan measured windows, cut cloth, hung new curtains, and carried out the burlap ones improvised by a New Age, Human Potential Movement girlfriend forty years ago. I told him the burlap had the sentimental value of remembered introduction to the guitar riffs of John Fahey. Earlier, she had taught me to dance the Twist. He held the ragged burlap in outstretched arms to limit the dust storm and mite-and-mote-induced sneezing, and muttered that forty-years-ago cuteness was irrelevant during the post-Aquarian age.

"Actually, forty-five years ago," I recalculated. "Lives in Bakersfield now. Married to a lawyer. Has a separate car for her two little dogs."

"Congratulations, Dad," Ethan said, and stuffed wads of burlap into a trash bag on the sidewalk, a brown haze rising above it.

Ann painted a trompe l'oeil pencil on a table, signing a corner of it. Judy suggested actually hanging the Haitian painting of funeral devils that was leaning against the wall, atop the rusted steamer trunk in which I store, the bones of adverse book reviewers. I expect my grandchildren will again refresh my dwelling décor on Russian Hill when I turn a hundred or so and need another makeover.

Funeral precisions are usually not exact; funeral processions are supposed to be stately and slow, because what's the rush? But in Haiti, the body on its litter or in its box is sometimes raced through the countryside with zigzag dodgings on the backs of sweating friends and relatives, so that the crowd of evil spirits — they only know how to move in straight lines — can't take possession. In nature, nothing grows in a straight line. Although evil spirits lurk everywhere, they are unnatural.

The peasants have a good point there on the mountainsides of Haiti, where rocks seem to grow through the night, no matter how often they are gathered and hauled away. We are works in progress as long as we are alive, trying for control, sometimes convinced we have control — *some* control — over who we are and where we are going and what might lurk on our path. We are also works in progress when we're dead, revised in the memory of those who remember, forgotten by those who forget, dodging oblivion as long as time continues, eventually disappearing into the gently sifting dust of other forgotten bedeviled souls. It's still a kind of joining, isn't it?

When the Messiah comes, some Jews believe the dead will rise and roll to Jerusalem, which is already crowded enough with Christians, Jews, Arabs, and a headquarters of Baha'i, including a busy cafeteria, without a sudden ingathering of every Jew who ever lived, clamoring for lox with their bagels. Aside from this earthly reward, the concept of a future heaven is weak in Jewish tradition, which is why we have to do the best we can on earth, *tikkun olam*, to heal the world and create the best approximation we can of heaven on earth, for others and incidentally for ourselves. When my old Aunt

Anna in Cleveland spoke of rolling to Jerusalem, I practiced skating on wooden wheels on the streets of Lakewood. I'm no longer waiting for the Messiah, roller-skating, or wondering if I can reserve a room at the King David Hotel.

This earth and this life are what we have, and sufficient. (In my opinion.) Perhaps we can make our Jerusalem, our heaven, by living in decency and kindness (not always possible), enjoying the appetites that nature has given us (and sometimes takes away), helping others, who also deserve decency, kindness, and appetite (except for those upon whom we need to exact revenge). *Tikkun olam* is what a person seeks, not merely forgiveness for sin and an eternal parole among angels. I believe my half-Jewish children have somehow absorbed this idea. When we hike in Muir Woods, they scramble off the path and down gorges to pick up trash, styrofoam and beer cans, even at the risk of poison oak.

Beyond survival, we mean to sing the song of our lives, make life shapely, fill it with feeling and meaning. The iPods in people's ears, the ducking and weaving to music, the rhythms of lovemaking express our hunger. Many die without achieving song in their lives. It's sad to see those whose days drone on and then just stop. They are not only unfulfilled; they are unfinished.

Death is the final masterwork achieved by everyone, but before the everlasting night, we look for love. Imperious, the moon hides itself. Sometimes it rises through pollen and pollution, yellow-gold and huge, seeming to burst with color — pollution part of the deal — before it rises further into cold white light.

Friends die. The "statistical miracle" became another statistic. Awake and asleep, in dreams and when I think I'm not dreaming, I remember that wife I loved, others whom I cared for and who are now gone. Unless there's a heaven where they stay forever, they don't remember me. If they are elsewhere, not in heaven, they are too busy to tend to fond recollections. When I remember them, I believe I'm keeping them alive. I can't expect the statistical miracle to do the same for me.

I lie awake before dawn and watch the sky brighten over San Francisco Bay, gulls swooping and honking their breakfast noises. Some of those who knew me, asleep in their own beds, still alive, liked me or didn't, disliked me or didn't, are now diminished into the struggle for mere existence, no more discovery or adventure in their programs, grateful for sleep, no more appetite for active liking or disliking. Without the reverberations of passion that keep us alert to others, my life today is not the life I remember. I also miss the presence of those who were indifferent to me, whom I thought I cared about not at all. I miss the departed who resented or despised me and to whom I returned this variety of caring. Perhaps I despised first, before their own invigorating snarls appeared. I miss a betrayer to whom I wished a state of permanent diarrhea, just another sweet dream I had — buried, he has no digestive rumblings at all. I miss our mutual spite. I even miss my first wife, from whom I fled for my life. For the aged, it can be lonely out here.

One night I dreamed of trying to lift the coins from my eyes, but of course I couldn't, because I was sealed by them, I was dead. That was vexing. They were *gold* coins, a joke about my name; I was supposed to spend them, not use them to press shut my days and nights. The coins were heavy and cold. How could I be dead, even dead in a dream, if I was able to make a schoolyard pun about my name, the one my father took because he had heard there was gold in the streets of New York?

I woke and there was only orangish nighttime conjunctival discharge sealing my eyes, to be washed away in warm water and not exchanged for goods or fun. Sleep is a dark hiding place pierced by flashes of light which blind as much as they reveal. We can't see much of what the dream shows us, and anyway, the dream may, like a friend or enemy, be lying. Dreams are just another part of real life, which also frequently deceives, part of the carnival midway down which we wander until we melt into the crowd, into thin and thick air.

The smells of the backyard after rain in Cleveland, the smell of verdant rot in the gardens of Canapé Vert in Port-au-Prince, the smell of fog fresh blown from the sea, sweeping over San Francisco in thermal turmoil, the smells of Melissa when I breathed her as we fell together into sleep — the smells of being alive, even if I'm no longer a child in Cleveland or a nosy wanderer in Haiti and Melissa is gone. When I leave the world, ashes packed into a container and then, like my brother Sid, distributed in handfuls in Muir Woods by my daughters and sons, I trust the ruling smell will be that of redwood leaves, branches, mulch. What a pleasure it is to breathe deeply of those smells. I'd prefer to be still there, but others will carry forward the privilege of gratitude and praise for delicious deep breathing.

Samuel Beckett, who understood about age as did his colleague Shakespeare, praised a randy impatience. "I can't go on. I'll go on." He took a somber pleasure in his grudging consent to living. A person might pretend to give up, and some do, but better if it's a feint, really, a fake-out. Just continue. Despair is okay if you employ it to compose a fine sui-cide note because you'll be too busy composing it to jump from the chair with the noose around your neck. Might as well predict the inevitable, accept it wholeheartedly, but take your time about finishing the long farewell which begins at birth. Like suicide intentions, many embraces end in not em-bracing. Terminal, I'd like to sit in the garden of the Hotel Oloffson in Port-au-Prince, lemonade to my right, notebook in front of me, reconciling myself to the imminent. I'll eat a papaya first.

We can't imagine a drop into nothingness, what happens to insects, animals, or fruit falling from the tree, without con-soling ourselves with a dream of everlasting heaven, as some do, or everlasting memory, as I do. When I look into the eyes of my children, I believe something of me will endure. When I looked into the eyes of the wife I loved, I knew it ab-solutely. But then life teaches us to stare at doubt, pain, loss; deal with it. Joy lurks somewhere. I discover a less oblivious zest than that which I found in moments of ecstasy. All must be saved, or maybe not.

A good weep, curled in the fetal position, tight in bed, sobbing noisily for lost love, followed by a dizzying bellyache crisis of laughter, rolling on the floor, in danger of letting go sphincters and valves — what's not to like about living? How not to be happy with the ebb and flow of things, even with the inevitable losses, even if they lead to the full stop?

When I asked my father how he was feeling, during lucid moments at the end of his long life, he regularly an-swered: "Fine, fine, fine." His aging and death were matters to be neither fought nor denied; they were merely facts in the world; he was fine. We who still live might learn to collaborate with a future of absence, dealing life into the picture, making a story or song of our passage, winning a less than full stop after the inevitable full stop. We can hang on, hang in there, creating our music and tumult, until the full stop in silence. Our pleasure and love may mark others remembering us.

When Death comes to claim me, scythe in hand, in his European white sheet drag or the black formal suit of Baron Samedi, the voodoo Guardian of the Cemetery, I'd like to roll back on my heels in the official stage gesture of surprise and hope the scythe does its work swiftly. The downside of that instant would be that I couldn't celebrate my farewell with Ethan, asking him to sing once again his country rock song from age nine ("My baby done left me, / So I went downstairs and ate some fried chicken"); couldn't tell Ari what bliss it was when he took charge of rationally organizing my beatnik pad; would be unable to remind Ann of how I fell with tears and relief into her arms in Israel after Melissa decided she needed to start life over without me; couldn't remind Judy of the time when she climbed onto an empty pedestal in a park in Cleveland and enacted a conquering four-year-old hero for Sid and me; wouldn't be able to repeat Nina's imitation of a cable car stalled on Russian Hill, backing up, making a running start. I'd prefer not to go swiftly if all these matters would remain undone. They probably will be.

Ethan, remember when we passed a rotting heap of vegetation and you said, "Dad? Make you homesick for Haiti?"

It's pleasant to think of immortality, or at least to be

recalled sometimes with love. I remember my old friends Francis Xavier, Victor, Harold, also those whom I cared for or disliked, in their good and bad times, their youth and age. In return, I want to be remembered, too. It's a version of heaven and hell, which some believe in. But like most of us, I suspect that when I'm gone, really and truly gone, I may be melted into air, into thin air.